MUSIC TO MOVE
THE SOUL

MUSIC TO MOVE THE SOUL

Steve and Ruth Adams

First published 2003 by Authentic Lifestyle

07 06 05 04 03 7 6 5 4 3 2 1

Authentic Lifestyle is an imprint of Authentic Media,
9 Holdom Avenue, Bletchley, Milton Keynes, Bucks, MK1 1QR, UK

Distributed in the USA by Gabriel Resources,
P.O. Box 1047, Waynesboro, GA 30830-2047, USA

British Library Cataloguing in Publication Data
A catalogue record for this book is available from the British Library.

1-85078-515-5

Cover design by Sam Redwood and Al Gray

Printed in Denmark by Nørhaven Paperback
Print Management by Adare Carwin

CONTENTS

INTRODUCTION

Why do hoards of young people part with significant amounts of money to frequent concerts and clubs every week? Why do they turn to their CD collection as a doorway for expressing the varied emotions they experience? And why, in Christian settings, do they often connect best with God during worship? It's simple: music moves the soul.

That is the understanding on which these 100 session outlines have been written. Young people listen to, think about and remember many of the song lyrics they hear. A song about drugs not working will often be more compelling than an adult saying the same thing. Songs make excellent teaching tools.

The majority (37) of the groups or artists featured in the book have record deals with secular labels. The remaining 13 are on Christian labels and are overtly Christian. This is deliberate. Using chart tracks as a means for communicating Christian truths allows you to re-contextualize a song in the minds of young people. If you teach on the subject of God's kingdom, using 'Turn', by Travis, the next time your young people hear the song on the radio they will recall what they learnt about God's kingdom. These sessions allow you to infuse secular music with spiritual meaning while drawing out some of the deeper messages.

It cannot be claimed that all the sessions reflect exactly what the artist or band intended to say through the songs they are based on. All songs are interpreted by the listener and assigned meaning that reflects their own personal views and experience. So it is here. While every effort has been made to remain true to the artist's apparent message, the songs are used as a springboard into looking at Christian living – something which many of the artists did not have in mind when writing.

Use the book as a one-off resource, picking sessions from time to time to tie into your wider curriculum, or run a 'music month', grouping four together on similar themes as a teaching series.

Some of the sessions in this book will require a small amount of preparation prior to the meeting. It is advised that each session be read through before being used in a group setting. Most of the sessions involve some Bible study and practical activities. Each one should provide enough material for a 45-minute meeting. They are geared towards 14 to 18-year-olds, but can be easily adapted for use with older, or younger, audiences.

Try to think around the subject you are looking at. Listen to the track several times before the session and get a feel for the message coming through. It's also worth investing some time in the venue you are meeting in. Soft seating or cushions, low lighting and a relaxed atmosphere will help young people relax – and therefore open up to the music and discussion.

Bible translations used in the sessions include NCV (New Century Version), NIV (New International Version) and The Message.

Your young people are likely to have many of the CDs used in the book, so you could borrow them.

1. SEIZE THE MOMENT

TRACK 6: Tā Moko

LENGTH: 5 mins 9 secs

IN BRIEF: A chance for the group to assess how they use their time and what they would do if these were their last 3 hours.

Album:
One Giant Leap
[Palm Pictures, 2001]

Artist:
Various

APPLICATION

This track raises a vital, but little thought-about question: *When you are laying on your deathbed, what do you think you might regret having not done, said or been during your lifetime?*

Before introducing the subject, explain that you are going to do a time survey. Hand out sheets of paper headed, 'My Average Day'. The sheets should be divided into three sections: morning, afternoon, and evening. Ask each person to fill in how they spend an average day. When filled in these should be put to one side for use later on.

If you had 3 hours left to live, how would you spend them?

Introduce the subject of seizing the moment by reading out a series of last lines which famous people uttered on their deathbeds. These can be found at: www.geocities.com/athens/acropolis/6537/real-b.htm

Before you start the track, you might want to explain a little bit about the '1 Giant Leap' project. Film-maker Jamie Catto set out in 2001 on a round-the-globe journey. He visited Senegal, Ghana, South Africa, Uganda, India, Thailand Australia, New Zealand and the USA. He took with him a digital audio camera and sought out the 'most happening musicians and thinkers' in a bid to explore unity and diversity. Visit www.1giantleap.tv for further details.

PLAY THE TRACK > > > > >

Divide those present into groups of two and give them 5 minutes to ask and answer this question to each other: *If you had 3 hours left to live how would you spend them and, if they were spent with people, what would you talk about?*

Allow for feedback from each pair. Almost certainly, everyone will have opted to be with people in their final few hours. Follow this up by telling them to refer back to the time survey they did earlier. Say to them that people are a priority for most of them. Most of them would want to spend the final hours of their life with their friends and family, not with their possessions. Are those people-priorities reflected in the survey of their average day?

Distribute a selection of teen magazines among the group and let them spend 5 minutes seeing how many references to death or dying are in their pages – there will probably be very few, if any. After they have shared results, ask them what the flavour or feel of the articles and news in the magazines is?

Explain that living for the here and now is what popular culture is about. It's about the 'buzz' of being young and experiencing the thrills of life. The Bible recommends this, but adds a note of caution – look to what's ahead.

Split the group into smaller clusters. Give each the following passage to read, and questions to answer:

Read Ecclesiastes 11:7-10 and chapter 12:1-5 and answer these questions:

- What do the passages instruct us to do regarding the 'dark days' or hard times? (v.8) Why do you think this is?

- How does the encouragement to live life to the full, in verse 9, and the warning that God will hold you to account for everything you do make you feel?

- How does the analogy of ageing (12:1-5) make you feel? Fearful or more determined to make the most of what you have now?

Sum up by referring to the call for us to live life to the full, but with a knowledge of God. End by playing the track again and inviting everyone to make a list of several things they want to do more of in order to ensure they give time to the things they know really are important.

2. THE KINGDOM OF GOD

TRACK 11: Racing Away

LENGTH: 5 mins 58 secs

IN BRIEF: This session looks at what the Kingdom of God is, where it is located and our part in bringing it about.

Album:
One Giant Leap
(Palm Pictures, 2001)

Artist:
Various

APPLICATION

This track provides a great springboard for looking at the subject of isolation in society and of God's ideal for his people.

PLAY THE TRACK > > > > >

Jesus calls his followers to be builders of the kingdom of God on earth

Play the first 25 seconds of the track, the section about TV, and then pause it. Ask the group whether they agree with what was said, and why.

Resume the track. > > >

At 2 minutes 37 seconds, there is a 40-second instrumental. During this, read Leviticus 19:32 and Matthew 18:5-6.

When the track has finished, tell the group that Jesus calls his followers to be builders of the kingdom of God on earth. Jesus said when he came that the kingdom of God was near. But what is his kingdom, and what does it mean for 'the elderly' and 'the children' mentioned in the song?

····> ····> ····> ····>

Divide the group into four smaller clusters. Give each group one of the sets of verses from a gospel below. Tell them to discuss what each verse says about the kingdom of God and jot down what they find out.

- ■ MATTHEW
  Matthew 5:10
  Matthew 7:21
  Matthew 13:33
  Matthew 19:14

- ■ MARK
  Mark 4:26-29
  Mark 10:15
  Mark 10:24-27

Where is God's kingdom located?

- ■ LUKE
  Luke 10:8-9
  Luke 13:20
  Luke 19:11-27

- ■ JOHN
  John 3:3
  John 18:36

Allow time for the groups to feed back what they have found out. Write their conclusions on a flip chart/OHP if available.

Draw to a close by raising the question: 'Where is God's kingdom located?'

Wait until someone gives the correct answer – that it's in the hearts of Christ's followers and that it becomes a tangible reality as they make it one.

Challenge them that they are the answers to the issues raised in the song: dealing with the lack of respect for the elderly in society, the lack of love for humanity and patchy care for children across the globe starts with us laying foundations for Christ's kingdom through our daily actions and choices.

End by asking each person to think of one way they are going to build God's kingdom in the coming week. Get an empty plastic bottle and spin it. Whoever it points to must explain to the rest of the group how they are going to build the kingdom in the week.

3. REJECTION

TRACK 5: So Unsexy

LENGTH: 5 mins 7 secs

IN BRIEF: A chance to explore how we deal with rejection and the example Jesus gave when he was rejected.

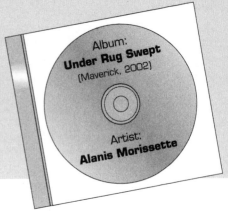

Album:
Under Rug Swept
(Maverick, 2002)

Artist:
Alanis Morissette

APPLICATION

All human beings tend towards one of two extremes when they face conflicts or challenges: they either take all blame and responsibility on themselves or they won't accept any responsibility and place all fault at the feet of others.

Get those present to identify which extreme they lean towards by reading the following. (Emphasise that this is just a preference – we may experience both extremes at different times):

> A friend invites you to a party at which you know no one. You get briefly introduced to one or two people but after 10 minutes, your friend disappears into the crowd leaving you alone. Do you:
>
> (a) Panic. Feel inadequate. Imagine no one wants to talk to you. Question why you are unable to make friends and enter a 'why am I so unpopular?' spiral.
>
> (b) Feel annoyed you've been left alone. Think your friend should have taken more responsibility for you and blame them for the fact you're now feeling like a loner. You set out to enjoy the party anyway.

Explain that rejection is hard, but we often make it worse by losing perspective and becoming irrational. We interpret the actions of others without knowing for sure what they were thinking. We take the message about us – which their actions suggest – on board and create a false view of ourselves.

PLAY THE TRACK > > > > >

12

When it's finished, read out the last line of the song which starts, 'these little rejections . . . ' Say that this is an important key to dealing properly with rejection. Allow for discussion around this and any other parts of the track people have picked up on.

Give each person these questions and Bibles (or Psalm 139:1-10 printed out), and invite them to think on their own for 5 minutes. Play the track again while they do this:

■ Are you more of a 'blame yourself' or a 'blame others' type of person? What effect does this have on you?

■ Read Psalm 139:1-10 and think about this: God knows you better than any one else ever will, but still makes a statement about your value by staying close to you.

■ When you feel let down, how do you react? Do you feel like giving up because you feel so worthless?

■ Do you agree with Alanis Morissette that rejection feels smaller when instead of 'abandoning yourself' you stick to what you know about the value God has placed in you?

Are you more of a 'blame yourself' or a 'blame others' type of person?

Allow for any feedback then say you're going look at how Jesus dealt with rejection. Read John 13:2-5, emphasising three things:

1. Jesus knew one of his close friends was rejecting him (v.2)

2. Jesus was able to carry on despite being rejected because he knew how God saw him and knew his place in God's plan (v.3)

3. Jesus didn't adopt what Judas thought of him as part of his own self-image.

End by drawing two columns on a flip chart/OHP. At the top of one write **'Rejection'** and in the other **'Reality'**. Brainstorm with the group how they feel as a person when they have experienced rejection. For each of these words, write in the other column what the reality is about you as a person, i.e. what God says.

4. FREEDOM TO EXPLORE

TRACK 9: You Owe Me Nothing in Return

LENGTH: 4 mins 56 secs

IN BRIEF: A look at the how much freedom we have in Christ to go exploring other ways of living.

Album:
Under Rug Swept
(Maverick, 2002)

Artist:
Alanis Morissette

APPLICATION

PLAY THE TRACK > > > > >

As a group, identify (using the words in the CD inlay) what you think is true of God in this song, and what is not.

Say that the track is about you having the freedom to explore and experiment and find out for yourself. It goes against the idea of having to choose a certain path, out of fear that you will lose the love of someone close if you go a different way.

The Bible explores both these ideas. Divide the group into two teams. One team must argue that God loves us whatever we do and that his mercy is boundless. The other must come up with arguments to support the case that God's mercy has conditions and expectations. Use these verses to get the teams going:

Boundless Mercy: Romans 11:29-32
Conditional Mercy: John 14:21

---> ---> ---> --->

Get the group in a circle and ask them:

- Do you think it is important to have a time in your life when you leave the path you were brought up on and 'explore' other ways of living?

- Can you really relate to people who have been 'off the rails' if you yourself have not been?

- Who in the Bible went off exploring and living it up for a while? (*The Prodigal Son*.) How did he cope in the long run?

- Does doing things differently have to be something that God is not part of?

- Do you think Christians have misunderstood Christ's message and made it more 'safe' than he meant it to be?

- What things that Jesus did might be rejected as too extreme by today's church if he appeared and did them next week?

End by saying that life, and scripture are not always as black and white as we'd like them to be. Encourage them to be willing to think through hard questions and talk to God about seeming grey areas.

Remind them that God's grace is what starts our relationship with him and that it begins on an unconditional basis: 'while we still sinners, Christ died for our sin' (Romans 5:8).

God's grace is what starts our relationship with him and it begins on an unconditional basis

5. THE BEATITUDES

TRACK 9: Blessed

LENGTH: 4 mins 2 secs

IN BRIEF: This session looks at the upside-down values of Jesus and how in God's economy we win by losing.

Album:
Rhythms of Remembrance
[Rocketown, 2001]

Artist:
Apt Core

APPLICATION

This track is based around the Beatitudes in Matthew 5. Using low lighting and scented candles, begin with the following meditation once the group is comfortable and settled:

> *Think of a swing. It could be one you played on as a child. Picture yourself swinging on it, building momentum and experiencing the excitement as you lean back and push forward. Feel the rush of swinging so high you know you can't let go. Feel the wind pushing against your face . . .*

PLAY THE TRACK > > > > >

Play the track. At 1 minute 21 seconds, after the words, 'they need to see' continue the meditation, reading over the words on the song . . .

> *To build momentum on a swing, to feel the excitement and the rush, you have to lean back in order to push forward. Many people believe that leaning back – being poor in spirit, showing mercy when it is not deserved, trying to be pure, recognising your weaknesses, hungering to please Jesus above yourself – is weak and will lead nowhere.*
>
> *Jesus said that the only way we really move forward is by pushing back. The only way we find ourselves, is by giving of ourselves and our energies to others.*

When the track has finished, display several traditional pictures of Jesus – the type found in some older Bibles, children's books and some Catholic shops. The images should portray Jesus as meek and mild. If you can't get hold of any, continue from here anyway.

Tell the group that many traditional pictures of Jesus' life over-emphasise his gentle side. However, the accounts we find in the gospels show Jesus modelling a challenging way of life – one that turned society's values on their head. He gave people the benefit of the doubt, promised to reward the poor not the powerful, said that those who were last would be first, said that those who were mourning would find joy again and promised that those who were hungry to know him would find him.

PLAY THE TRACK AGAIN > > > > >

Play the track again and ask the group to pick one of the descriptions that are mentioned. You may want to read or write them out before you start the music:

Blessed are . . .

The poor in spirit – theirs is the kingdom of heaven.

Those who mourn – they will be comforted.

The meek – they will inherit the earth.

Those who hunger and thirst to do right – they will be filled.

The merciful – they will be shown mercy.

The pure in heart – they will see God.

The peacemakers – they will be called sons of God.

Those who are persecuted because they do right – theirs is the Kingdom of Heaven.

Encourage them to meditate on the one they pick and think about how they can begin to infuse that value into their life.

Open it up for discussion using these questions as a springboard:

- ■ 'Blessed are the poor in spirit, for theirs is the kingdom of heaven'. Can you think of any people who have modelled this in their lives? What does it look like?

- ■ What does it mean for us, in contemporary life, to lay down our life in order to find it again? In what areas of life is this hardest?

- ■ Are there times you can recall when you have tried to model upside-down values? How did this feel?

- ■ Does laying our lives down in order to find them mean that we become doormats? Think about how Jesus acted when challenged

6. APOSTLES' CREED

TRACK 1: *Creed*

LENGTH: *3 mins 20 secs*

IN BRIEF: *A look at what the Apostles' Creed is and what it says about the pillars of the Christian faith*

Album:
Rhythms of Remembrance
[Rocketown, 2001]

Artist:
Apt Core

APPLICATION

Explain that you are going to look at the Apostles' Creed and think about what makes a Christian a Christian. Make these points to introduce the subject.

- ■ The 'Apostles' were early church leaders (2 Corinthians 11:5).

- ■ Jesus chose the Apostles and gave them the job of making disciples of the world (Matthew 28:19).

- ■ Apostle means 'messenger' or one sent to convey a message. (NB: some church streams apply different meaning to their modern-day 'apostles'.)

- ■ The Apostles' Creed sums up the key beliefs of those who follow the Christian way – the seven key pillars of Christian belief:

  1. Jesus Christ as God's son
  2. The Holy Spirit
  3. The Church
  4. The communion of saints
  5. The forgiveness of sins
  6. The resurrection of the body
  7. Life everlasting

PLAY THE TRACK > > > > >

At around 55 seconds into the song, a recital of the Apostles' Creed, laid over electronic drumbeat, begins.

Use these questions as a springboard into discussion on what makes a Christian a Christian:

■ Jesus said that by people's fruit – the way they live, who they are and the effect they have on others and the world – you would be able to tell whether they were believers. How do key Christian beliefs (above) affect and translate into fruit in people's lives?

■ Are core beliefs, such as these, important? Why?

■ What is the difference between an essential and non-essential belief? How do you know which is which?

Give out paper and pens and ask people to list the seven key beliefs (above) in priority order from the one they find easiest to believe, to the one they are most uneasy with.

Ask people to select one of the key beliefs listed – preferably the one they are most uneasy with and to consider what difference this belief should make in their lives. What fruit should it bring about in them? Challenge them to spend some time this week researching and thinking about that key belief.

What is the difference between an essential and non-essential belief?

7. OUTWARD APPEARANCES

TRACK 3: Sk8er Boi

LENGTH: 3 mins 23 secs

IN BRIEF: This session raises the question of whether we take the time to look beneath the surface and find the qualities that lie beneath in others.

Album:
Let Go
(Arista, 2002)

Artist:
Avril Lavigne

APPLICATION

This track is an engaging story of a baggy-clothed skater boy and a budding ballerina. Outward appearance suggested the boy would not date the girl but, as the song highlights, outward appearances can be deceiving. This session advocates looking beneath the surface and not judging by appearance only.

Start with a game, helping the group to assess how much they judge people by their outward appearance. Set up four empty boxes, labelling one **'Geeky'**, one **'Cool'**, one **'Brainy'** and one **'Nerdy'**. Give out teenage fashion and culture magazines to the group. Instruct them to cut out as many pictures of people (of any age) as they can. As a group, they must then decide which of the four boxes each picture should be placed in. As the group allocates a box, ensure they state the reasons for their selection. What was it about the people placed in the **'Geeky'** box that suited them to that box?

Use several fruits to illustrate that judging on what we see outwardly can be dangerous. Have a coconut, a banana and an orange on display. Ask for words to describe what the outside of each of the fruits look like.

Then say that, in human terms, a banana with its bright skin and long, slender shape might be described as a 'cool and attractive' person. The sweet smell of an orange might make 'fragrant' an apt word for it – if it was human. In human terms, what sort of person might the coconut be? Allow for suggestions – based only on its outward appearance.

PLAY THE TRACK > > > > >

Use the following lyrics from the song, and the questions, as discussion starters on the subject of looking beneath the surface:

'Too bad you couldn't see the man that boy could be.'

■ Do you ever feel that people don't see the potential in you?

■ Do you ever feel that you don't take the time to see the potential in others?

'There is more than meets the eye. I see the soul that is inside.'

■ Is it easy to see what's inside people?

■ What stops you seeing the heart and soul of others and not just the label they are wearing?

■ What are some practical things you can do to make sure you see what's inside and not just what's outside people?

'Sorry girl but you missed out.'

■ Have you ever felt you misjudged someone or didn't see the potential in them?

Take the coconut in your hand and ask what's most important in a fruit – how it looks or how it tastes? Use a hammer to break the coconut. Explain that the coconut is like many people – nothing to turn heads outwardly, but beautiful, refreshing and with lots of goodness on the inside. Remind them that a fruit is judged primarily by its taste – by what is on the inside.

Tell the group you are going to look at the story of David. Explain that Samuel had been told by God to go and appoint the next king. Read 1 Samuel 16:6-13.

Ask the group how they think God sees them? Like they see each other? Re-read verse 7 and emphasise that God sees our heart and motives as much as our hair, faces and what we are wearing.

FAKING IT

TRACK 2: Complicated

LENGTH: 4 mins 4 secs

IN BRIEF: This session looks at the masks we put on and the ways in which we 'fake it' in front of others.

Album:
Let Go
(Arista, 2002)

Artist:
Avril Lavigne

APPLICATION

This track talks about when we fake it and put on masks, pretending to be something we are not.

Ask the group to think whether anyone has ever said to them, or implied by the way they treated them, that they liked them just the way they are. How did this make them feel?

Try to get hold of a Rubik's Cube. You can order them from: www.rubiks.com or simply print off a picture of a cube from this site.

Explain that we are like a Rubik's Cube in that we each have many different faces and sides. Like a completed Rubik's Cube, we sometimes show just one side of ourselves. At other times, like a muddled Cube we display different bits of our character and feel like we are not very sorted people. At other times, when we are very self-conscious, we might cover up our true colours, instead displaying the colours we think people will be impressed by.

We each have many different faces and sides

PLAY THE TRACK > > > > >

22

Use the following line as a discussion starter:

'You become somebody else round everyone else'

- ■ Is this true of you?
- ■ Can you identify any masks you wear?
- ■ What does Jesus say about having confidence in the person he has made us?

Take a close look at the parable of the Pharisee and Tax Collector in Luke 18:9-14. Ask a volunteer to read out the parable.

Raise the following points/questions. You may wish to split into groups to do these:

- ■ For whose benefit was the Pharisee speaking? Who did he want to hear him?
- ■ For whose benefit was the Tax Collector speaking? Who did he want to hear him?
- ■ Think about who you live for and what motivates you. Is it the praise of people around you or the fact that God sees how you live?
- ■ Re-read verse 11. The Pharisee was trying to make himself look better by putting others down. Do you do that?
- ■ What would have happened if someone far more important had arrived as the Pharisee was praying? How would he have felt?
- ■ How do you think the Pharisee treated his friends? Were they just an object for him to use to make himself look better?
- ■ While the Pharisee got his identity from how he rated next to others, the Tax Collector looked to God to see his real identity. Who was on firmer ground? Why?
- ■ Look at verse 14. Who was God pleased with? How can this encourage us if we feel like the Tax Collector – useless and a bit downtrodden?

End by encouraging the group to take confidence in God's confidence in them. Encourage them to work hard to let the real them shine through and to take confidence in God's promise in Joshua 1:5.

9. BORN AGAIN

TRACK 3: Born Again

LENGTH: 4 mins 40 secs

IN BRIEF: This session aims to help people express what being 'born again' means in a culturally relevant way.

Album:
Have You Fed The Fish?
(XL Recordings, 2002)

Artist:
Badly Drawn Boy

APPLICATION

Start by asking the group these questions:

- What does the phrase 'born again' mean to you?
- What might the phrase 'born again' mean to someone who had never been in a church or met Jesus?

Ask one person to pretend to be an average non-churched, non-believing young person you might meet in the street. Ask another member of the group to try to explain what being 'born again' means and their experience of being a born-again Christian.

Before they start, take the person playing the non-believing youth aside and instruct them to listen very carefully to words that the born-again person uses. They should challenge them on any words that would not be understood by someone who had never been to church. They should also ask hard questions about what being born again really means.

Let several pairs have a go at this. It will challenge the group to think very carefully about the words they use and way they explain their faith.

PLAY THE TRACK > > > > >

Pick up on the line from the song that talks about the reasons for being born again, and says 'the more I look, the less I find'. Say to the group that people who are not born again are not interested in an abstract presentation of the gospel. They want to know why you are born again on a personal level. The song raises the questions: 'Maybe there's a reason why I'm born again'. Spend 5 minutes thinking about the real reasons why you are born again. Be honest.

After they have done this, suggest they work in pairs talking to each other about the reasons why they are born again. The rules are:

1. Their reasons must be personal, not abstract.

2. The way they explain it must use language that would make sense to un-churched young people.

Look at the account of Paul in Athens in Acts 17:16-28. Ask someone to read it out and make these points:

■ The Good News was alien to the people (v.18). This is the same situation as today.

■ Paul starts his explanation of the gospel with something they are familiar with (v.23). He roots it in their culture.

■ Paul keeps using language and references to the Athenian culture that the people of Athens would have easily understood (v.28).

Say that not only do our explanations of being born again need to be personal, but they also need to be rooted in language and culture which un-churched people understand.

Spend a few minutes brainstorming analogies for being born again, using popular culture: films, books, computer games, sports, music, technology etc. You should spend time thinking up some before the meeting to stimulate the group. Examples include:

■ Being born-again means knowing there is a greater force at work even when life is very hard. The Lord of the Rings film trilogy highlights this principle.

■ Being born again means I communicate with God. This is like Internet chat rooms. I can't see the person I'm talking with, but they are real and they speak to me.

Play the game you tried at the start, with the non-believing youth and the born-again believer. This time the born-again person should make it personal, explaining reasons why they are born again, using easily understood language and analogies from popular culture.

10. THE BURNING BUSH

TRACK 8: CentrePeace

LENGTH: 1 min 52 secs

IN BRIEF: A chance for young people to reflect on Moses' experience at the burning bush and what God might be asking of them.

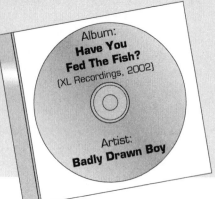

Album:
Have You Fed The Fish?
(XL Recordings, 2002)

Artist:
Badly Drawn Boy

APPLICATION

The track has no lyrics and should be played on a loop as the group uses the meditation below.

This session will require some setting up, but will provide a great opportunity for young people to spend time in reflection. You will need 5 bags of sand (more or less depending on the size of the group), and a plastic sheet to spread the sand on. This is all available cheaply from DIY stores.

Set up the sheet on the floor and spread the sand out so there is enough space for the group to sit on the sand. Place cushions around the edge and use candles and low lighting to help create a reflective atmosphere. Have Bibles handy.

PLAY THE TRACK > > > > >

Listen for God in your thoughts and in the things you look at

You're standing on holy ground – God is here

Give out copies of the following meditation to the group and invite them to spend the next 30 minutes reflecting on the issues raised in the meditation.

Moses saw that though the bush was on fire it did not burn up. So Moses thought, 'I will go over and see this strange sight – why the bush does not burn up.'

When the Lord saw that he had gone over to look, God called to him from within the bush, 'Moses! Moses!'

And Moses said, 'Here I am.'

'Do not come any closer,' God said.

'Take off your sandals, for the place you are standing is holy ground.' (NIV)

What made the ground holy? It was God's presence there

You are standing on holy ground – God is here.

This is your desert space

It's a space for you and God.

This is the place where God wants to connect with you as he connected with Moses.

Take off your shoes as a sign that you recognise God's holiness and want to show him respect. As you feel the connection of your feet on the sand reflect on the connection of your soul with God. He is closer to you than your foot is to the sand.

Listen to God's voice.

Expect to hear him. He will speak to you like he spoke to Moses.

Pick up some sand in your hand. How many grains are there? One thousand? One million? God knows exactly how many grains there are. He knows every detail about your life and your experiences.

Spend some time here.

Listen for God in your thoughts and in the things you look at.

Feel the connection with him.

Read the story of what God was calling Moses to in Exodus 3:7-14 and what he achieved through Moses in Exodus 12:31-36. Ask God what he is calling you to.

As you leave, keep the connection live. God's fire will burn on and, like the bush, it will not go out.

11. ACCOUNTABLE FRIENDSHIPS

TRACK 7: *Whenever*

LENGTH: 3 mins 53 secs

IN BRIEF: *A look at the importance of accountability in friendships.*

Album:
Trailer Park
(Deconstruction, 1996)

Artist:
Beth Orton

APPLICATION

Introduce the theme with a game. Put stickers on everyone's back without telling them what is written on them. Using a different word for each person, utilise both good and bad characteristics such as grace, honesty, love, compassion, greed, envy, selfishness, etc. Tell the group that their word will be either a good or bad human characteristic.

The object is to discover the word written on their back by asking other people questions about it. Questions can only be answered with a 'yes' or 'no'. When someone has discovered their word, they should sit down.

Make the point that we need the advice of our friends because they see us from a different angle and can point things out to us about ourselves that we could not otherwise see.

Ask the group which characteristics they think are important in a friend. Write the ideas on a flip chart or OHP.

Note whether anyone suggests 'honesty' as an important characteristic. Try to draw out their thoughts on this using the questions below:

- How importantly do you rate honesty in your friendships?

- Has a friend ever been honest with you about something negative they see in you? How did this help you get a better perspective on yourself? Did it hurt?

- How often do your friends speak honestly to you about negative things they see in you, which you can't see yourself?

- Do you find it easy to be honest with a friend about something they clearly can't see but which they need to work on for their own good?

Select two people and record each of them on tape reciting a nursery rhyme. Play the tape back and ask the person who was recorded whether they think they sound on tape like they do in real life. They will more than likely say no. Then ask the rest of the group. They will probably say yes.

Make the point that our view of ourselves is distorted simply because we are not able to separate from our bodies and get a wider perspective. The fact that we think we sound different from the way we really do shows us that we need to listen to what others say about us and not assume we have perfect perception of ourselves.

PLAY THE TRACK > > > > >

When it has finished, make reference to the level of openness referred to in the friendship described, and how the singer says that anything she asks, her friend can ask of her too.

Explain that the word for this level of friendship is accountability. An accountable friendship is not about one person listing all the faults of the other, but of a mutual willingness to let the other share their perspective on the areas in their friend's life that are strong and those that need work.

Split the group into two and give one of the following passages and questions to each, to spend 15 minutes studying:

Rehoboam rejects good advice: 1 Kings 12:1-13

- What was good about the way King Rehoboam handled the peoples' question? (verse 5-6)
- What reaction did the King's actions provoke? Read 1 Kings 12:18-20.

David and Jonathan: 1 Samuel 20:1-9

- What evidence is there here of the depth of friendship between David and Jonathan?
- How did Saul react? How important was it that David trusted Jonathan? Read 1 Samuel 20: 24-33.

Ask each group for feedback on what they read. Draw the session to a close by getting everyone thinking about how they can make their friendships accountable.

12. FEELING EMPTY

TRACK 11: Galaxy of Emptiness

LENGTH: 10 mins 7 secs

IN BRIEF: A look at the things we fill our lives with.

Album:
Trailer Park
(Deconstruction, 1996)

Artist:
Beth Orton

APPLICATION

Start with these questions:

- Do you ever feel empty inside? Why?
- Do you think God can fill the emptiness we feel? How?

PLAY THE TRACK > > > > >

The first 3 minutes 45 seconds is instrumental. During this read the following meditation:

How big do you feel?

Do you see yourself as a giant or a dwarf in your environment?

Even the biggest, most powerful and influential person is like a single grain of sand in a desert when put in perspective next to the galaxy.

Our galaxy – or star system – is around 100,000 light years across. Most galaxies contain around 100,000 million stars and astronomers describe the galaxies that are nearest to each other as being in 'local groups'.

Where does it all end? Does it end?

The nearest star to earth is 25 million miles away.

In the southern hemisphere, there is a star that is one million times brighter than the sun, but is so remote that it cannot be seen without a telescope.

This puts us into perspective. It also puts the size and power of God, who created all of this and is present in all of this, into perspective.

From 8 minutes 45 seconds, there are no more lyrics, just a further 1 minute 23 seconds of music. During this, read Matthew 10:29-31.

Give each person an empty box and say that the box they have represents their life. From birth, we all start to fill our lives with things: hobbies, activities, people, sports. Ask them to spend 5 minutes writing down on slips of paper the things that fill their life and place them in the box as they do.

When this is done, boxes should be passed to the person on their left ready for that person to add further slips of paper.

Ask volunteers to read out the following verses: Ezekiel 36:26; Matthew 7:11; John 14:27; Luke 22:19; Romans 5:5; 2 Corinthians 5:5; James 1:27. Everyone should note down from the verses what God wants us to fill our lives with and add slips of paper to the box they have been passed. Encourage them to add other ideas, even though they may not have been read out.

Boxes should be passed back to the right and people given 5 minutes to read through things that have been added. Play the track again while this is happening.

End by producing a box which you have previously filled to the top with bits of paper so that there is no room left for anything else. Explain that if we fill our lives so full with activities, possessions and friends, there can be no room left for Jesus. We need to make sure there is space for him.

We need to make sure there is space in our lives for Jesus

13. WAITING FOR GOD

TRACK 8: Waiting for the Blessing

LENGTH: 6 mins 1 second

IN BRIEF: An opportunity to look at the subject of time and how God wants us to deal with things he has asked us to wait for.

Album:
Roller Coaster
(Kingsway, 2002)

Artist:
Brian Houston

APPLICATION

Have a clock with a second hand (showing seconds) on view as people arrive. Introduce the session by asking everyone to watch the clock, in silence, until you tell them otherwise. Allow about 3 minutes to go by – or enough time for the group to get fidgety. Then ask them the following:

- How did it feel watching time go by? Did time seem to go slower?
- Did they use the time in any way other than just waiting for it to go by?
- Were they bored?

Introduce the theme of waiting for God, for his blessing and for him to respond to our prayers.

Split the group into two teams. Do the following Time Quiz. In the 2-minute rounds, allow 2 minutes for each team to write down their answers then ask each team to read out their answers, awarding points to the winners. During the quick-fire rounds, anyone in either team can shout out the answer as soon as they think they know it.

2-MINUTE ROUNDS

1. Write down as many secular or Christian songs as you can which have the word 'time' in.

2. Make as many words as you can, of any length, out of the letters T, I, M, E.

3. Add together the ages of all the people in your team. Include months, weeks and days. (You may need to provide a calendar for this.) The winning team is the one with the highest total age.

QUICK-FIRE ROUNDS

1. How old was Methuselah – the oldest man in the Bible – when he died? (*969 years*)

2. Complete the phrase: 'The time of your . . . ' (*life*)

3. What two words describe a diagram showing a person's parents, grandparents and other previous generations? (*family tree*)

4. Name the film starring Tom Cruise in which people are arrested on the basis of crimes they will commit in the future. (*Minority Report*)

PLAY THE TRACK > > > > >

Play the track and invite the group, as they listen, to think about any things they are waiting on God for.

Repeat the 'watching the clock' exercise done at the start. This time instruct them to use the time to prepare. Tell them that after 3 minutes they will need to have come up with their favourite three (pop/dance/worship etc.) songs of all time. After 3 minutes, go round the room and let everyone name their three favourite songs.

ASK:

- Did the time go quicker than before, or slower?

- Did you focus on the clock as much? Were you so aware of time passing?

Explain that when we are waiting for God to do something we often put other things on hold. When you all watched the clock at the start you were focusing only on that, not using the time for any other purpose. The Bible teaches three things about when we are waiting for God to do something for us:

1. God has made 'everything beautiful in its time' (Ecclesiastes 3:11, NIV). In other words, different things in our lives have a right time when they will happen.

2. God does not want us to put everything on hold while we wait for something we have asked him for to happen. The Bible says that, 'hope delayed makes the heart sick' (Proverbs 13:12, NIV).

3. Sometimes God does not grant things straight away because he wants us to learn by waiting. The answer given to Paul was 'no' because God wanted him to learn to depend on Christ more (2 Corinthians 12:8-9).

Allow time for God at the end. Play the track a second time and invite people to talk to God about things they are waiting for.

14. SAYING THANK YOU

TRACK 10: Your Whisper to My Soul

LENGTH: 8 mins 32 secs

IN BRIEF: This session aims to help young people assess things that stop them being thankful, and to say thank you to God.

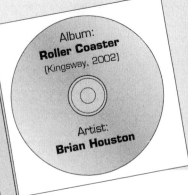

Album:
Roller Coaster
(Kingsway, 2002)

Artist:
Brian Houston

APPLICATION

Select two people. Explain that you have a gift for each of them. Give the first person something which, when compared to what you give the second person, will seem small. You could use a Snickers bar and give person number 2 a giant Cadbury's bar. Ensure you allow time for person 1 to respond to you when you give them the present. Note whether they say thank you. Note their, and the group's reaction, when you give person 2 a similar, but notably larger gift.

Ask these questions:

- To person 1: How did your feelings change from when you received your gift to when you saw the gift given to person 2?

- To person 2: How did seeing the smaller gift given to person 1 make you feel about your larger gift?

- To the group: How did your feelings change about the gift given to person 1 when the larger gift was presented to person 2? Was this fair?

Tell the group that sometimes how we feel about something we receive from God – whether a material or spiritual gift – can be altered when we see a similar but seemingly better gift given to someone else. In this session, we are going to think about why it is important to look at what God gives us without looking at things he is giving to others around us.

PLAY THE TRACK > > > > >

Play the track and ask the group, as they listen, to think about things that stop them being thankful.

Produce a clear drinking glass and a bowl of water. Read, or memorise and paraphrase, the short meditation below, following the instructions in brackets:

Imagine this glass is your heart.

God designed it to be filled with an attitude of thankfulness.
(Fill the glass to overflowing with water.)

Think about things in your life you are thankful to God for.
(Allow several minutes while they think.)

Other things frequently fill our hearts and push out the attitude of thankfulness. (Drop some small pebbles into the glass.)

Think about things that push your thankful attitude out.
(Allow several minutes of thinking time.)

The way we get to a place of being thankful is by asking God to open our eyes to everything he has given us and not let ourselves compare them with what he's given to others.

David wrote Psalm 23 to express his thanks to God. Listen to it being read and use it as a stimulus to thank God.

(Read Psalm 23 slowly.)

Think about things in your life you are thankful to God for

15. I WANNA BE

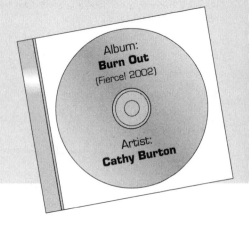

TRACK 1: Don't Wannabe

LENGTH: 4 mins 30 secs

IN BRIEF: A look at what young people do and do not want to become.

Album:
Burn Out
(Fierce! 2002)

Artist:
Cathy Burton

APPLICATION

Start by asking the group what they want to be or do in life.

After one or two have shared their thoughts, ask them what they don't want to be or do in life.

PLAY THE TRACK > > > > >

Explain that another way to start thinking about what you want to become, is to identify the things you don't want to become. Refer to the song lyrics in the CD inlay and highlight some of the things listed there that the singer doesn't want to be: stuck in the middle, a gossip, kicked around, etc.

Give out pens and paper to each person. Play the track again in the background and give them 5 minutes to think about how they don't want their future to look – what they don't want to be or do. Encourage them to be specific. Suggest categories of:

What I don't want to be in my

(a) school/employment

(b) friendships

(c) relationship with God

(d) church

After 5 minutes say that you are going to look at a case study of someone who became what they didn't want to be – Samson.

Split the group into three smaller groups. Give each a section of the story to read and then present to the whole group:

- GROUP 1: Judges 13 – Samson's supernatural conception and mission is laid out by God.
- GROUP 2: Judges 15 – Samson begins to defeat the Philistines.
- GROUP 3: Judges 16 – Samson loses his way because of Delilah.

After the groups have presented their sections ask these questions:

- In Judges 13, God said his plan for Samson was to deliver Israel from the Philistines. Did Samson fulfil this? Why, or why not?
- What was Samson's fatal mistake?
- What does this story say about the importance of our decisions in how our futures pan out?

Draw the session to a close by bringing the focus back towards God and setting aside 5 minutes for the group to consider what they do want to do and be for God.

PLAY THE TRACK AGAIN > > > > >

Read Judges 13:5. Tell the group that as well as knowing what we don't want to become, we need to know what we are heading for. In the same way that God had a plan for Samson, he has plans and hopes for their lives. Ask them to write down anything they feel or have felt God wants them to do or be for him – however silly it might seem.

Before the meeting, ensure you have enough envelopes for each person present. Invite them to place the sheet they wrote their 'don't want to be' thoughts on in the envelope along with the sheet listing anything they feel God wants them to do. Ask them to seal it and address it to themselves. Collect these up and tell the group you will post them back to them in six months.

16. A NEW PERSPECTIVE

TRACK 11: Belongs to You

LENGTH: 4 mins 48 secs

IN BRIEF: An opportunity to look at life from a different perspective.

Album:
Burn Out
(Fierce! 2002)

Artist:
Cathy Burton

APPLICATION

This song of commitment and dedication to Jesus is about realising that everything you are and own does in fact belong to him.

You will need several sets of free-standing stepladders for this session, although chairs will do if ladders are not available.

Introduce the theme of perspective and say that the Christian faith is, in its simplest form, about giving your life to Christ and allowing him to stand you in a different place to the majority and give you a new perspective. Read Luke 24:30-31 as an example of how the disciples saw things very differently when Jesus 'opened their eyes'.

Give the following examples and invite the group to think of situations from their own experience where they have seen things from a different perspective:

- A shop attendant thinks you gave her £20 when in fact you gave £10. She gives you £15 change for a purchase of £5. You decide in your heart to be honest because you know it is God who gives and takes wealth anyway, and you know he is calling you to honesty.

- Your friend's parents are about to loose their home due to unpaid debts. You have been praying for God to help. An unexpected legacy is received and the parents talk about lucky coincidences. You see it differently – you clearly see God's hand in it.

Take the stepladders (or chairs) and lead the group out onto the street, or to the local shops if there are any. Ask them to climb the steps and observe the world for a few moments from this different perspective.

When you have returned, feed back on how things looked different. Draw parallels between that and how Jesus gives us a new perspective.

Ensure everyone is comfortable and relaxed. Pray the following prayer as an introduction to the track:

> Lord, you opened the eyes of your disciples to see you.
> Douse us in your Holy Spirit. We want to see things as they really are.
> Everything that we are or that we own belongs to you.
> Sometimes we struggle to really mean that, but we open ourselves to you.
> Come and help us discover that you are all, in all, through all.

PLAY THE TRACK > > > > >

Play the track and encourage the group to meditate on it.

Allow for several minutes of silence when it ends. Repeat the prayer above, then play the track again.

PLAY THE TRACK AGAIN > > > > >

Christian faith is, in its simplest form, about giving your life to Christ

17. AFRAID?

Album:
Kingdom Come
(Re:think Records, 1999)

Artist:
Charlie Peacock

TRACK 7: Don't Be Afraid

LENGTH: 3 mins 50 secs

IN BRIEF: A chance to look at things we are afraid of and unpack the effects of being afraid of things on our lives.

APPLICATION

Have a bucket-sized container on display at the front of the room. Place inside photocopied sheets with two columns, one headed **'The Fears that Only I Know About'** and the second headed **'How I Will Face Up to These'**. Cover the bucket with a paper 'lid' taped round the edge.

PLAY THE TRACK > > > > >

Ask whether they could relate to any of the common fears raised in the song. Ask one or two leading questions and allow time for people to talk about any of their own fears, which the song touched on.

Ask for a volunteer to model the effect that being afraid has on people. Seat the person on a stiff-backed chair in the centre. Appoint a scribe and initiate a brainstorm of things people are afraid of. As the scribe notes the ideas, others in the group should gaffa-tape the ideas onto the seated volunteer. Plenty of tape should be used to ensure not only that the bits of paper are stuck on, but also that the person is gradually fixed to the chair.

When the person is covered in slips of paper, and taped securely, invite them to explain how they feel. Draw a parallel between the way they feel – paralysed – and the effect that the fears, which they are now covered in, have on us when they go unchecked.

To round off the illustration, cover the person stuck to the chair in a sheet and, as you do, explain that things we are afraid of restrict our freedom. We often try and hide from these things. However, this doesn't make the problem go away it just makes it seem more severe and it becomes all we can focus on.

Follow this up by asking everyone to think specifically of one thing they are afraid of. What effect does this fear have on them? How does it alter their actions? Are there things that they avoid doing, or places they avoid going to because of it?

Have three buckets on display. Label the first **'People Who Were Afraid in the Bible'** and type out multiple copies of the following verses, placing them in the bucket:

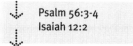

Genesis 3:10 (Adam)
Exodus 2:14 (Moses)
1 Chronicles 13:12 (David)
Luke 22:44 (Jesus)

Label the second bucket **'What People in the Bible Did When They Were Afraid'** and type out multiple copies of these verses:

Psalm 56:3-4
Isaiah 12:2

Label the third bucket **'What God Says to Us When We Are Afraid'** and type out multiple copies of these verses:

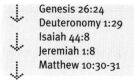

Genesis 26:24
Deuteronomy 1:29
Isaiah 44:8
Jeremiah 1:8
Matthew 10:30-31

Tell the group that the next 10 minutes are for them to bring things they are afraid of to God. Tell them they can use the three buckets for this purpose. Explain there are verses in the buckets relating to what each bucket is labelled.

The things we are afraid of restrict our freedom

Draw the session to a close by inviting a volunteer to break the seal on the bucket that was at the front and give out the sheets inside. Play the track a second time as people fill in some of the fears only they know about on the sheet and then fill in the second column listing how they plan to face up to these. Encourage them to use the verses they read, above, to help them gain the confidence to face their fears.

Close with prayer, using 1 John 4:18 as a focus.

18. LOSERS WINNING

TRACK 2: Wouldn't It Be Strange

LENGTH: 4 mins 3 secs

IN BRIEF: A look at the 'upside down' teaching of Jesus that the losers will in fact be winners.

Album:
Kingdom Come
(Re:think Records, 1999)

Artist:
Charlie Peacock

APPLICATION

Start the session by saying there are some things in life that seem strange and appear to make no sense. Use paper folding as an illustration of this. Lay out six pieces of paper of all different sizes – from a five-pound note size to an A3 size – or bigger. Invite guesses on how many times people will be able to fold the different pieces in half.

You will find that any piece of paper, whatever its size, can only be folded in half six times. Let the group try, then say that some things seem one way but in reality are another. This was a big part of Jesus' teaching. Ask if anyone can think of things, ideas, accepted teachings or principles that Jesus turned on their head.

Play a game to demonstrate one of Jesus' key principles: that the apparent losers are in fact the winners. Split the group into two teams. Each team is given several newspapers to use as wind pumps along with one paper fish per person. Cut these out from paper ensuring they are all of a roughly equal size. On the word 'go', one player from each team must propel their fish from one end of the room to the other using only the wind power created by flapping the newspaper onto the floor. When one person reaches the finish line, the next person in their team can start. Explain that the object of the game is to be the first team to get all the fish to the end.

However, when the game is over read out Matthew 20:16 and award a prize to the losing team. Then ask:

- How did that make each team feel?
- What did Jesus mean by this teaching?
- What does this say about Jesus' view of position and of people?

Explain that Jesus was looking at the motivation in people's hearts and saying that those who are hungry to be first will in fact be last, while those who are happy to put others first will themselves get moved to pole position.

PLAY THE TRACK > > > > >

Play the track, and then pick up on the following points raised, using them as discussion starters:

- Do riches really make you poor? In what sense?

- In what ways might power make you weak?

- What would motivate you to 'welcome your defeat'? In what ways did Jesus welcome what appeared to be his defeat?

Emphasise that what Jesus is advocating is a whole different approach: a turning upside down of how we have been tuned to think and live. Read Matthew 5:3-10 and Matthew 19:30 several times over with the track playing quietly in the background. Let it sink in. Close by challenging the group to think about what this teaching means for them this week.

Those who are hungry to be first will in fact be last

19. HISTORY MAKER

TRACKS 2, 3, 4 & 5: In Dust We Trust

LENGTH: 15 mins 35 secs in total.

IN BRIEF: This session is designed to be done in a church building that has been a site of worship for some time. It helps young people explore their place in the Christian story and God's presence throughout time.

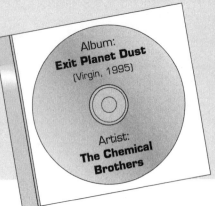

Album:
Exit Planet Dust
(Virgin, 1995)

Artist:
The Chemical Brothers

APPLICATION

The four tracks run together well. They provide a very contemporary dance sound contrasting the material being studied, which explores faith through the ages.

PLAY THE TRACKS > > > > >

Give out copies of the meditation, below, and instruct each person to take their time as they work through it:

Place the palms of both your hands flat on the floor in front of you. Feel the stillness and solidity of the floor.

For hundreds of years, ordinary people have met together to pray and connect with God on this piece of ground. Let that thought soak in.

> *How many thousands of prayers have been said here?*

> *How many worries have been expressed?*

> *How much joy and sadness has there been?*

The faith in God you have is something much bigger than you.

Through those years, millions of trees have grown, died and been succeeded by new ones. Animals have been born, lived and died. Seasons have come, and gone. And people have lived, had experiences, and died.

The only person to have watched and experienced it all is our Father – God, who made history and is involved in it. This may make you feel insignificant or it may make you feel secure.

The Bible says that God sees everything, in every situation: every minute, hour, day, month, year, century and millennium. And he is emotional with it. When he sees you struggle, he wants to stand with you, like a friend.

The Bible says:

> 'You know where I go and where I lie down.
> You know thoroughly everything I do.
> Lord even before I say a word,
> you already know it.
> Where could I go to get away from your Spirit?
> Where can I run from you?
> If I go up to the heavens, you are there.
> If I lie down in the grave, you are there.'
> (Psalm 139)

In another thousand years, followers of Jesus may remember us on this piece of ground, as we remember people before us. People won't remember what mobile you had, your first car, the type of perfume you wore, the logos on your clothes or where you went on holiday each year. The stuff which will last is the response you make to God's call to you. God sees your history in those terms. He wants to be your history maker.

What follows is an account of Saint Augustine of Hippo, a man who lived 1,600 years ago. He is remembered for his love for God's grace. Before you read on think about this: If someone remembered you for something 1,600 years from now, what would it be?

> St Augustine of Hippo was born in AD 354 in North Africa. He had an able mind with many questions about life which he sought answers to. He dabbled in the oriental religion of Manichaean but found it provided no answers to the questions which fascinated and troubled him – namely his search for the ultimate truth. At the age of 29, he moved to Italy and took up a professorship. There he met the Bishop Ambrose who impressed him. One day in AD 386, he was struck while reading Romans with the answer to his question – Jesus was the way to truth and salvation.
>
> He withdrew to the country and became a follower of Jesus. He returned to Africa, gave all his possessions away and devoted himself to serving God.
>
> He went on to become a pastor and Bishop believing that the inner state of human spirituality – the secret heart of a person – was a mirror of the divine presence of the creator. In making the world, God had partly imagined himself in it and in making the human heart, he had particularly imagined himself.
>
> The key to Augustine's life and faith was that Jesus was the answer to his questions about the ultimate truth and real meaning in life. He knew Jesus was his hope and that new life was a gift – and not earned.
>
> Augustine saw God's grace before, during and behind every human action. He was a Doctor of Grace: he was convinced that the grace of God, through Jesus Christ – the man and God – was the only thing that could save him.

Close your eyes and think about your place in the Christian story. Saint Augustine's legacy was grace. What will be yours?

20. THE LORD'S PRAYER

TRACK 8: One Too Many Mornings

LENGTH: 4 mins 13 secs

IN BRIEF: This session offers a different approach to the Lord's prayer, helping young people engage with each section of it.

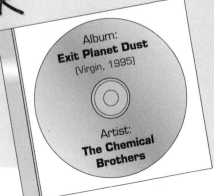

Album:
Exit Planet Dust
(Virgin, 1995)

Artist:
The Chemical Brothers

APPLICATION

PLAY THE TRACK > > > > >

Start the music and set it on a loop so that it repeats. Have the group sit in a circle and set up in the centre a trinity candle (a candle with three wicks – available from most candle shops). Don't light the candle yet.

Ensure the lights are dimmed and that there is a relaxed atmosphere. Provide cushions so that people are comfortable.

Start to read the Lord's Prayer from Matthew 6:9-13. Read each line slowly and with meaning, allowing time for the group to digest the meaning. Repeat each line several times before moving onto the next.

Allow several minutes silence after reading the prayer. Then light the candle and say, 'Father, Son and Holy Spirit hear our prayers to you. Come and meet with us. We open our hearts to you. Holy Spirit, convict, teach and change us. Jesus, illuminate our hearts with your life-example and teaching. God, father us and enfold us.'

Repeat the Lord's Prayer inserting these phrases at the indicated places:

- ■ After reading verse 9: There is power in your name Jesus. Thank you for changing us.
- ■ After reading verse 10: Teach us and help us to do your will on earth.
- ■ After reading verse 11: We receive everything you give us with thanks.
- ■ After reading verse 13: When we are tempted help us to run to you.

Close by blowing out the candles. As you do, the smoke will rise up. Tell the group that God has heard the prayers they have said. Like the smoke, they rise into the air and God hears them.

Father, Son and Holy Spirit hear our prayers to you.

Come and meet with us. We open our hearts to you.

Holy Spirit, convict, teach and change us.

Jesus, illuminate our hearts with your life-example and teaching.

God, father us and enfold us.

21. TANGLED UP LIVES

TRACK 6: Trouble

LENGTH: 4 mins 30 secs

IN BRIEF: An opportunity to reflect on times we put our foot in it and tangle up our lives and relationships.

Album:
Parachutes
(EMI, 2000)

Artist:
Coldplay

PREPARATION

You are going to create a tangle-web, which you will need to mark out before the meeting. Draw out on the floor a web along the following lines: mark a spot to represent the centre using masking tape. Draw a hexagon (6-sides), using masking tape, around the centre measuring about 3 metres from edge to edge. Draw another, larger, hexagon whose edges are about a metre from the edges of the first hexagon. From each point on the outer hexagon use masking tape to draw lines to the centre.

Just inside the edges of the second hexagon write out the following verses relating to confession and forgiveness on slips of paper: James 5:16; 1 John 1:9-10; Luke 6:37-38; Matthew 6:14-15. Also, print copies of these instructions:

> *Spend a few minutes reading the verses and reflecting on whether you need forgiveness or whether you need to forgive someone. Make a note of anything that comes to mind then move onto the inner hexagon.*

Just inside the edges of the inner hexagon write out, on slips of paper, the following verses about living right: 1 Corinthians 13:4-7 and Galatians 5:22-23. Print out these instructions:

> *Once we have confessed our sin to God and to those we have hurt, God calls us to pursue love in the way we deal with others. Read the verses and spend some time asking God to give you his love.*

At the centre write out, on slips of paper, the following verses relating to intimacy with Christ: John 15:4-5 and John 16:12-15. Print copies of these instructions:

> *Intimacy with Jesus and walking with his Spirit is the best safeguard against doing things we later regret. Read the verses and meditate on your relationship with God.*

Split the group into lads and girls. Send one girl and one lad out and instruct the rest to form a circle in their gender groups, holding hands and facing inwards. Explain that they must get as tangled up as they can by moving behind, around, under or over each other, using legs and arms and bodies, but still holding hands.

When they have done this call in the two you sent out and explain that their job is to untangle their team without allowing any of them to let go of each other's hands. When you say 'first move', each of them can give their team one instruction (e.g. Sally, move under Sarah's right arm and turn around to face her). Repeat this, calling second, third fourth move etc. until one of the teams has untangled. Award a prize for the first team to untangle.

Explain that this illustrates how our lives are often tangled. We say or do things that we don't mean to and create a tangled web of relationships.

PLAY THE TRACK > > > > >

Unpack some of the following lyrics, using them as discussion starters:

- 'I never meant to cause you trouble'. Do we mean to put our foot in it? If not, what is it that leads us to put our foot in it?
- 'A spider's web, I'm caught in the middle'. What similarities does a fly in a spider's web bear to us when we mess up and get caught in a situation?
- 'So I twist and turn'. Is this how you react when you put your foot in it?

Explain to the group that when we mess up, God wants us to face up to what we have done and deal with it. We can then move on and grow in our faith. Give each person pen and paper.

PLAY THE TRACK AGAIN > > > > >

Play the track again and ask everyone to start the tangle-web at the outer edge. They should spend some time reflecting on the instructions and reading the verses before moving onto the inner hexagon, and finally the centre.

End by challenging them to act on anything they noted down during their time in the web.

22. SALT AND LIGHT

TRACK 3: Spies

LENGTH: 5 mins 18 secs

IN BRIEF: This session helps young people consider the importance of being salt and light.

Album:
Parachutes
(EMI, 2000)

Artist:
Coldplay

APPLICATION

Have Matthew 5:16 projected onto the wall using an OHP or PowerPoint for when the group arrive. Also, have a bowl of salt and enough candles for one per person in view.

Brainstorm:

- Ways in which Christians are called to be like salt and candles *(have a distinct flavour, provide light, etc.)*.
- The qualities of light.

PLAY THE TRACK > > > > >

Play the track and make the point that sometimes as followers of Jesus it can feel like we are fugitives, or that there are spies secretly watching us and how we live.

Read Matthew 5:13-16.

Ask the group to move into pairs and give them 5 minutes to brainstorm things that Christians do or say that they think make non-Christians take note. This can either be from their own experience, things they have seen or just ideas in their heads. Feed back and share the ideas.

Explain that people are always watching each other. We dress the way we do based on what celebrities and fashion designers decide should be in the shops this year. We ask other people's opinions on music, films and sports personalities. We want to know where people are going out. Everyone is looking at everyone else. For Christians, this can be a good thing – if we use the opportunity wisely.

Ask volunteers to read out the following scenarios:

1. You are about to start a fight with someone in your year who has trodden on your lunch. People are gathering round, excited about the impending ruck. As you square up, a lad from the year above steps in. He gives you his lunch and manages to prevent the fight.

2. You are about to start a fight with someone in your year who has trodden on your lunch. People are gathering round, excited about the impending ruck. As you square up, a lad from the year above steps in. He suggests that you both have the fight on the field rather than in the school hall.

ASK:

- Which of these is most likely to happen?
- Which of these would intrigue people the most and get people thinking?

Close by giving each person a candle and some salt to take away. Light people's candles, saying that God has put his light in us and, if we use it wisely, other people will see its brightness and be intrigued.

Sometimes as followers of Jesus it can feel like we are fugitives

23. DISTANT FROM GOD

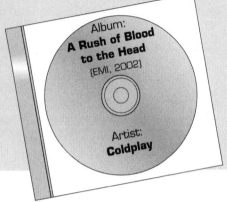

TRACK 8: Warning Sign

LENGTH: 5 mins 29 secs

IN BRIEF: An opportunity to explore some of the warning signs people get when they get distant from God.

Album:
A Rush of Blood to the Head
(EMI, 2002)

Artist:
Coldplay

APPLICATION

Start by dividing the group into an even number of teams – each team should have two or three people in. Label half the teams 'A' and half 'B'. Each A team should find a B team to partner and then go to opposite ends of the room. Give each pair of teams a makeshift phone made out of two yoghurt pots with string tied between them. The further apart the teams are the better. If you can use a garden, make the string between the pots as long as possible. Give all the A teams a list of words. Give each team the same list but with the words in different orders. Use the following words, or add your own, sticking to the theme of communication: hearing, listening, understanding, direction, misunderstanding, blurred.

Once each team has pulled the string tight and practised listening and speaking down the 'phone' line, start the game. The object is to be the first A team to correctly communicate all the words down the line. The B teams should write them down as they hear them. The A teams must not say the words so loudly that the team at the other end can directly hear.

Explain to the group that listening like that can be like listening to God: it is not always clear and sometimes we aren't exactly sure what he's saying. Sometimes it can seem too much effort and we start to drift or switch off.

PLAY THE TRACK > > > > >

Comment on the ways in which this song can reflect our relationship with God:

- It refers to 'warning signs' that the relationship is not what it should be.
- The chorus says, 'the truth is I miss you' which is how we can feel when we switch off from God.
- The person is referred to as 'an item to discover' which reflects how it is with us and God.
- The track relates how one person passed the other one by. We sometimes do that to God.

Give out paper and pens and give everyone 3 minutes to write their own list of warning signs they get when they start getting distant from, or switching off to God.

Give them a further 3 minutes to write a list of things that commonly distract their walk with God.

Feed back what people have written down. On a flipchart, write down what people listed as things that commonly distract them from God. Go down the list, asking the group to suggest what these things bring into their lives e.g. fun, laughter, a way of forgetting about real life etc. and add these suggestions next to each one. Contrast these with the things God brings into their lives.

Suggest to the group that sometimes we don't listen to God and we forget about all the good things he brings into our lives. Distractions seem to offer more tangible pleasures, but they can blur our focus on God.

Read Genesis 3:1-7 and ask:

- Did Adam and Eve forget what God had said? If not, what made them eat the fruit?
- What was the consequence of Adam and Eve eating the fruit?

End by playing the track again and inviting people to use it as a stimulus to pray to God, to tell him they are missing him if they have become distant and to do what the final line of the song says: 'to crawl back into your arms'.

Before they leave, tell them to remember the warning signs they came up with and to act on them when they appear.

24. FEELING OUT OF CONTROL

TRACK 11: Amsterdam

LENGTH: 5 mins 19 secs

IN BRIEF: This session looks at where God is when we feel life is out of control.

Album:
A Rush of Blood to the Head
[EMI, 2002]

Artist:
Coldplay

APPLICATION

Start by playing Twister with a twist – smear the board in fairy liquid. Depending on where you are, you may need to put down an old sheet under the Twister board.

After the game, talk about the fact that playing the game like that made them feel out of control. Life is often like that too. We feel out of control and unable to deal with situations in the way we would like to.

Pick two volunteers. Instruct one to try to keep a straight face at all costs and the other to try to make them laugh. They can use props, sing, shout or do whatever they want, but must not actually touch the person. Play a couple of rounds with different people.

Say that as well as often feeling out of control, although we can try very hard to hide our emotions, as in that game, we can only keep a hold on our emotions for so long – eventually they will seep out.

PLAY THE TRACK > > > > >

Draw attention to the line that talks about being 'dead on the surface', but 'screaming underneath'.

Ask if anyone in the group can remember their most out-of-control day, where everything seemed to be manic and they felt out of control. Allow a couple of people to share.

Give out sheets of A4 paper and pens to everyone. Ask them to divide their paper into quarters and write the following headings in the boxes:

BOX 1: Situations Around Me that Make Me Feel Out of Control.

BOX 2: Things I Do That Make Me Feel Out of Control.

BOX 3: Things I Do that Make Me Feel More In Control.

BOX 4: How I React When I Feel Out of Control.

Divide the group into pairs and allow 10 minutes for discussing answers to these questions and to fill in sheets.

Come back together and invite anyone who wants to, to share what they wrote.

Divide the group into three teams. Tell them they are going to look at Psalm 46. The first team should look at verses 1-3, the second team look at verses 4-6 and the third team look at verses 8-10. Each team should have the following questions in mind as they look at their section:

■ What do these verses say about me?

■ What do these verses say about God?

■ What do these verses say about life when it seems out of control?

Give each team a chance to feed back their findings.

Close by playing the track again. Draw attention to the following line: 'You came along and cut me loose'. Encourage everyone that God is in even their most manic day.

25. DISTRACTIONS

TRACK 10: Raining in Baltimore

LENGTH: 4 mins 40 secs

IN BRIEF: A look at the role that distractions have in our lives.

Album:
August and Everything After
(Geffen, 1993)

Artist:
Counting Crows

APPLICATION

Introduce the theme by asking who delays doing the things they don't want to face, and who prefers diving straight into the difficult task.

Buy several bags of coloured M&M sweets. Choose three colours and pick out all the sweets of those colours. Divide them into two bowls, each having the same amount of sweets. In each bowl, place one single red M&M. Place the two bowls slightly apart at one end of the room, and two empty bowls at the other end.

Split the group into two teams and explain that the game involves members of each team running, one at a time, from one end of the room, where the empty bowl is, to where their team's bowl (full of M&Ms) is, at the other end. Each person must pick out one sweet and return it to their team's empty bowl at the other end using a straw. They must create enough suction through the straw so that the M&M stays on the end of the straw while it is moved. The next runner cannot go until the M&M has been placed in the bowl. Instruct each team the colour order that you want the M&Ms transferred in. When all colours are back, the single red M&M must also be collected. The winning team is the first to transfer all their sweets to the other bowl.

Explain that that game was like life. The really important things in life are like the single red M&M, they get crowded out very easily by all the other attractive pleasures and pastimes. We sometimes spend less time on the things that count in life (like the red M&M) than we do on the mass of less important distractions.

PLAY THE TRACK > > > > >

When the track has finished, read from the last verse of the song, which starts, 'I need a phone call', down to the end of the song. Explain that the character in the song is filling his time with distractions – thoughts of buying a car, listening to music or dreaming of what could be.

Split the group into smaller clusters of three or four people. Give each group the following questions to answer:

- ■ What distractions pop into your mind when you are trying to avoid facing up to something?

- ■ Draw up a list of things you often want to avoid, or delay dealing with in life.

- ■ Do you ever feel like avoiding God? Why?

Feed back as a group.

Explain that you are going to do a Bible study looking at what scripture says about distractions. Look at the following passages and answer the questions listed as a group:

1. Martha gets distracted: Luke 10:38-42

- – When you are with Jesus, how much do you listen and how much do things distract your attention?

- – What is the 'one thing' that Martha needs in v.42?

2. Fixing our eyes on the unseen: 2 Corinthians 4:17-18

- – Why, according to this passage, should we deal with difficult things that face us, head on? (v.17)

- – Draw up a list of things that are 'seen' (TV, computer games, hobbies etc.) and 'unseen' (Jesus, character, love etc.) in your life. Look at the 'seen' list and write 'temporary' across them. Look at the 'unseen' list and write 'eternal' across it.

3. Throw off distractions: Hebrews 12:1-3

- – What is the key in this passage to not growing weary and losing heart?

- – The writer refers to 'witnesses' as a means to spur him on. Are there people around you who are an example to inspire and spur you on?

Give everyone a red M&M. Read out Hebrews 12:2 inviting people to eat the M&M as a sign that they want Jesus to be most important in their life.

26. REAL LOVE?

TRACK 5: Anna Begins

LENGTH: 4 mins 31 secs

IN BRIEF: This session helps people understand what they want from a relationship and the characteristics they would look for in a partner.

Album:
August and Everything After
(Geffen, 1993)

Artist:
Counting Crows

APPLICATION

Have a spread of popular culture magazines laid out on the floor. Invite the group to spend 5 minutes looking through them at how love and boy/girl relationships are depicted. Spend a few minutes feeding back.

PLAY THE TRACK > > > > >

Play the track and follow it up by reading the first and fifth verses from the CD inlay. Use these as discussion starters around the question 'Is he really in love?'

Say that for celebrities there is a pressure to be seen to be dating. For us too, there is a strong desire to be in relationship with someone of the opposite sex. However, sometimes the desire to have a boyfriend or girlfriend can overshadow the part of us that evaluates whether a relationship is really going anywhere. We're going to do a quiz to help us understand better what we see as important in a partner.

Give out pens and paper and explain that the three answers to each question should be put in priority order. The aim of this is to help them get more of a picture of the kind of things they would look for in a partner. Read out each statement and get everyone to write answers individually:

My ideal partner is ...

1. MY IDEAL PARTNER IS

(a) funny
(b) intelligent
(c) caring

2. MY IDEAL PARTNER LIKES

(a) films
(b) walking and the outdoors
(c) reading and discussing

3. MY IDEAL PARTNER VALUES

(a) a big salary
(b) a big car
(c) a big group of friends

4. MY IDEAL PARTNER IS

(a) sporty
(b) academic
(c) an adrenalin junkie

5. MY IDEAL PARTNER

(a) spends their spare time working with the homeless
(b) spends their spare time at the gym
(c) spends their spare time with me

6. MY IDEAL PARTNER

(a) is forgiving and understands my quirks
(b) is generous with their money
(c) loves computer games

Split the group into two. Taking it in turns, each team sends one person to the leader who gives them a word from the list below. All the words relate to relationships. They must describe it to their team without using the word itself. The winning team is the one to get through the list first.

LISTENING   COMPROMISE   ADVENTURE   KINDNESS   TALKING

DISAGREEMENTS   INTIMACY   UNDERSTANDING   DISCOVERING

Which of the words best describes how they see relationships?

End by telling them to look back at the list of things they wanted their ideal boyfriend or girlfriend to be. Challenge them to spend time becoming that sort of person themselves.

27. THE LIFE OF JESUS

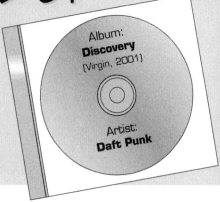

Album:
Discovery
(Virgin, 2001)

Artist:
Daft Punk

TRACKS 10 & 11:
Voyager and Veridis Quo

LENGTH: 9 mins 29 secs in total

IN BRIEF: This session provides a chronological walk through Jesus' life to help assess what events in Christ's life mean today.

APPLICATION

Do this outside or in a large house/hall. Set up the time-line, described below, using masking tape or string. Mark the start, end, and the stations along the way. The stations should be set up in chronological order along the time-line, as they are below. Copy out the verses in full. Photocopy the application sections as they appear below, providing several copies for each station. Have the music playing in the background as they walk the line.

PLAY THE TRACK > > > > >

Station 1: JESUS' BIRTH
Luke 1:26-33

Think about how Mary must have felt when the angel visited her: surprised, afraid and overwhelmed.
What things has Jesus asked you to do in your life? God gives us important things to do. He asked Mary the teenager to carry his son.
Like her, we can feel afraid and overwhelmed. Listen to the angel's words to Mary and let God speak to you: 'Do not be afraid. He is with you.'

Station 2: JESUS' BAPTISM
Luke 3:21-22

The Holy Spirit rested on Jesus in the form of a dove. The dove is a symbol of peace.
Let the Holy Spirit rest on you and bring you peace.
Be empowered for what he is calling you to do this week.

Station 3: JESUS' TEMPTATION Luke 4:1-13

There are many things that stand to tempt us every day.
What things are currently tempting you? Try to identify them.
Tell God what you are struggling with.
Trust that he will help you and give you strength to resist these temptations like he did for Jesus.
Think about the line in the Lord's prayer: 'Deliver me from temptation'.
Speak it over in your mind as a prayer to God.

Station 4: JESUS' ENTRY INTO JERUSALEM Luke 19:37-38

How would you greet Jesus if he arrived here now?
How would you feel?
What would you do?
Jesus promised he would return. He tells us to be ready.
What does this mean for you? How ready are you?

Station 5: JESUS CLEARS THE TEMPLE Luke 19:45-46

If you are a disciple of Jesus then your body is a temple of the Holy Spirit.
Think of your body as a house of prayer.
Jesus was angry because the people were misusing his house of prayer – the temple.
We need to develop a passion like Jesus displayed for protecting the places where the Holy Spirit resides in us.
Is there anything in your life that would upset Jesus?
Do you treat your body in a way that would make the Holy Spirit pleased to live there?

Station 6: THE LAST SUPPER Luke 22:14-16; Luke 22:27; John 13:4-5

What is your answer to the question Jesus asked about who is more important – the one at the table or the server?
Jesus was teaching his disciples a lesson in serving. He demonstrated that it's more important to serve than to be served.
How have you been served by others this week?
How have you served others this week?
How did being served, and serving make you feel?

Station 7: JESUS AT GETHSEMANE Luke 22:41-42

Jesus struggled with the same things we struggle with – he did not want to suffer.
He did not choose to die on a cross, but did it as an act of obedience to God.
Is there something you are going through at the moment which is causing you to suffer?
Have you asked God to take it away?
You are feeling what Jesus felt.
Focus on Jesus' words 'not my will, but yours'.
In your situation, can you identify what God wants as opposed to what you want?
Can you pray that prayer Jesus prayed?

Station 8: THE CRUCIFIXION Luke 23:44-49

Think about why Jesus died.
He had done nothing wrong but was taking the punishment for everything everyone else had done wrong.
The irony is clear: the only man to ever walk the earth blameless ended up taking all of the blame.
Today that might be called a miscarriage of justice.
But it wasn't a miscarriage because justice was done.
Jesus paid the price and you live because of it.
Spend time thinking about this and thanking Jesus for his death.

Station 9: THE RESURRECTION Luke 24:1-8

Imagine how the women felt on the way to the tomb.
They might have wondered whether Jesus had been delusional talking about rising from the dead.
Imagine how they felt when they saw the angels.
Have you met Jesus lately?
A one-off meeting isn't enough – we need to meet him again and again.

28. WORKING ALL HOURS?

TRACK 4: Harder, Better, Faster, Stronger

LENGTH: 3 mins 44 secs

IN BRIEF: An opportunity for the group to explore the pressures of work and career and see principles God laid down for working.

Album:
Discovery
(Virgin, 2001)

Artist:
Daft Punk

APPLICATION

Start by giving out pens and paper and asking people to put the following in priority order for their own lives:

- ■ Seeing friends, going out and having a laugh.
- ■ Doing well in your career.
- ■ Spending time with family.
- ■ Pursuing hobbies and interests.

Invite people to feed back and explain the order they placed these in. Ask the group how we show something is important to us. Make the point that we give time to what we value.

PLAY THE TRACK > > > > >

Play the track, and then ask what the group made of it. Explain that in today's society there is pressure in many jobs to work harder, better and faster, and to devote more and more of yourself to your career.

Look up the account of creation in Genesis chapter 1 and Genesis 2:1-3. Explain that you're going to spend some time reading through the account to find principles of how God worked during creation.

Read round as a group using the 'And God said . . . ' sections to indicate where the next reader starts. After each section, stop and discuss any principles you find about work.

Close by making these suggestions and challenging them to make these principles part of their lives:

- God put his all into the work he did. He set us an example of thoroughness.
- God took his time over the work he did. He didn't rush it.
- God did work that was good (Genesis 1:31).
- God enjoyed creation. He was pleased with it.
- God rested on the seventh day. He made it clear that rest was essential alongside work (Genesis 2:1-3).

In today's society there is pressure in many jobs to work harder, better and faster

29. DRY AND THIRSTY

TRACK 9: Honest Questions

LENGTH: 3 mins 30 secs

IN BRIEF: An opportunity to look within — at the soul — and to feed and nourish our inner selves with Jesus.

Album:
Gotta Get Thru This
(Polydor, 2002)

Artist:
Daniel Bedingfield

APPLICATION

Start by explaining that the track they are about to listen to relates to hard and dry times in life and about someone (God?) pouring their water down on a 'bruised and broken soul'.

Try to create a calm, meditative atmosphere using candles, cushions and soft lighting.

PLAY THE TRACK > > > > >

ASK:

- Have you ever asked God whether he really knows you like you've always been told he does?
- Have you ever whispered against God?
- Have you ever experienced God pouring his water (presence) on you when you felt dry?
- What do you think causes us to feel dried-out inside?

Explain that sometimes when we feel dry, empty and far from God it's because we have failed to nourish ourselves. Say that you are going to do two meditations to help them identify how well they receive God's nourishment.

For each meditation, opposite, you will need to photocopy or print enough for one per person. Instruct the group to read and reflect on the meditations on their own, and then to think through the questions honestly. For 'Roots', you will need a loaf of bread for the group to break from and eat as part of the meditation. For 'Rest' you will need a Bible for each group member. Play the track in the background while they are doing the meditations.

Allow plenty of time for the group to really engage with the meditation. Come back together as a group after each meditation and discuss the questions raised in the meditation.

1. ROOTS

This meditation looks at how well we draw in nourishment for our souls and from where.

Think about a tree. A large oak tree or an apple tree. Think about its roots. Its roots wind under the earth, away from the glare of human eye, underground, in the silent, quiet places. You don't see a tree's roots but they are its source of life, its being, its connection. If the roots stop growing, the tree stops growing.

The human soul is like the roots on a tree. It needs to be fed and watered, or it will stop growing.

Roots often mirror the shape of a tree's branches above ground. The human soul is like this. Jesus said that our mouths speak what our hearts – our souls – are full of. If you feed and water your inner soul, the outer you will flourish. If you neglect your soul, you will wither.

Like the soul, a tree's roots draw in whatever it finds to feed the tree. If the water in the ground is toxic, the tree will be poisoned.

What do you feed your soul with? How often do you feed it?

Think about these words. Identify any that you feel you lack:

silence	passion	honesty
meditation	forgiveness	peace
joy	relationship	Jesus

Our souls need these things to grow.

Break a piece of bread from the loaf in front of you. Imagine that the bread is not just food for your body, but also food for your soul. Imagine the bread represents and symbolises the thing(s) you identified as needing.

Eat the bread and use it as a symbol before God that you want to open your soul to him and be nourished.

2. REST

This meditation provides a chance to replenish the soul and invite Jesus to pour his water into us:

Take some deep breaths in and long breaths out.

Use this breathing prayer to help you:

Breathe in: love
Breathe out: hate
Breathe in: joy
Breathe out: worries
Breathe in: peace
Breathe out: stress
Breathe in: rest
Breathe out: bustle

Identify things crowding you that make it hard for your soul to find rest.

Put them to one side and turn to Psalm 23 in the Bible. Read it slowly.

Read the psalm again and really focus on the words.
Rest here for as long as you need to.
Read the psalm until it seeps into your soul.
Reflect on his love . . .
It is unfailing.
It will always be with you, all the days of your life,
from this very moment to tomorrow, to next week, to next month, to next year.
Forever.

What do you think causes us to feel dried-out inside?

30. BLOWN IT

TRACK 1: Blown it Again

LENGTH: 3 mins 20 secs

IN BRIEF: This session looks at the tongue and how it speaks from the things we've filled our hearts and minds with.

Album:
Gotta Get Thru This
(Polydor, 2002)

Artist:
Daniel Bedingfield

APPLICATION

Introduce the session by saying: Computer programmers use the term GIGO (Garbage In Garbage Out) to deal with problems in computer systems. If the computer outputs garbage, it is only because a human programmed garbage in. It is similar with us. If we consistently 'blow it' in what we say, it is because of what we have been filling our hearts and minds with.

PLAY THE TRACK > > > > >

Play the marshmallow game. Pick two contestants and sit them opposite each other. Ask questions to both. The person who fails to raise their hand first and answer the question each time must then insert 5 marshmallows into their mouths. Keep score and award a prize to the one who answers the most questions.

---> ---> ---> --->

Just as the marshmallows will rot the teeth, some things we absorb rot our minds and hearts

Tell the group that what we put into our minds through what we watch on TV, the films we see and the magazines we read seem sweet like the marshmallows. However, just as the marshmallows will rot the teeth, some things we absorb rot our minds and hearts. This causes us to say things we don't mean to.

Get volunteers to read Matthew 12:33-36 and Matthew 15:8-10, 18.

Give out paper and pens and instruct each person to draw up four lists labelled: 'TV', 'Magazines', 'Friends' and 'Places'. In the appropriate column they should list what they watch, read, who they spend time with and where they go. Then, they should mark the things that are healthy for their mind and heart with an apple symbol and those which rot them with a chocolate bar symbol. Tell them to take these sheets away with them and use them to analyse what they need to work on.

Sum up by reading out James 3:1-12 and reminding them that what we say comes out of what we have filled our hearts and minds with.

End by apple bobbing. Invite them to eat the apple they manage to bite as a symbol to God that they want to fill their hearts with healthy things.

What we say comes out of what we have filled our hearts and minds with

31. HOLDING BACK

TRACK 12: *Driving With the Brakes On*

LENGTH: 4 mins 42 secs

IN BRIEF: An opportunity to look at what makes us hold back from showing love to others. This session involves drawing and painting on sheets and would suit a large venue. Paints, marker pens and clay are required.

Album:
Twisted
(A&M Records, 1995)

Artist:
Del Amitri

APPLICATION

Briefly introduce the four kinds of love:

- ■ EROS: The love between a male and female in a romantic relationship.
- ■ STERGOS: Affection and mutual love between family members.
- ■ PHILOS: Brotherly or sisterly love. Love between friends.
- ■ AGAPE: Commitment and choice to do good to and bless another – the kind God shows us.

Brainstorm with the group some of the things that cause people to hold back from showing any of these types of love.

Send a fairly confident member of the group out of the room. Warn them before that what happens might freak them out, but that it is an illustration of what being open and vulnerable in love means.

Explain to the others that they must not touch the person, but can do anything else to freak them out when they return, from blowing on their face to whistling in their ear. Tell them on your signal to be ready to catch the person as they fall backwards.

Call the person back in. Blindfold them and position them to stand with their arms outstretched in a scarecrow position. Signal to the group to be quiet, apart from doing things to confuse the person such as blowing on them. After a minute or two ask the blindfolded person to lean backwards and fall. Tell them to trust that they will not be hurt. Ensure the group are lined up to catch them.

Remove the blindfold invite the person to explain how they felt.

Explain that the biggest thing that makes us hold back from really showing love to others is our fear of making ourselves vulnerable and of being hurt. It can feel like we are the blindfolded person – wide open to being hurt. However, it's in those times that we can also be rewarded the most for our openness when, instead of hurting us, the people we feel vulnerable with show love back – like when we caught the blindfolded person.

Read out the chorus from the CD inlay and ask:

- Can you relate to these images?
- What does it do to friendships when we hold back in them?
- How can you let the brakes off?

Suspend several large sheets just off the ground. Have some clay available. Read out 1 Corinthians 13:4-7 and explain that you want them to creatively interpret one of the characteristics of love, through drawing and painting on the sheet, or by creating a sculpture with clay. Encourage them, as they do this, to bear in mind the idea that love does not have its brakes on. Allocate a characteristic from the passage to each person and get them started. Play the track as they create.

Sit around in a semi-circle facing the sheets and sculptures. Draw the session to a close by giving out the following verses about love and asking people to read them out as a lead-in to a time of prayer, reflecting on the artwork and the messages it is conveying.

1 John 4:18
Proverbs 10:12
Ephesians 3:19
Romans 13:8
Matthew 5:44
John 15:13-17

What makes us hold back from really showing love to others is our fear of being hurt

32. POVERTY AND THE PRESS

TRACK 1: Food for Songs

LENGTH: 3 mins 37 secs

IN BRIEF: To help young people look beyond the images and messages given to them by the press when it comes to poverty and suffering.

Album:
Twisted
(A&M Records, 1995)

Artist:
Del Amitri

APPLICATION

This track deals with the reality of poverty and injustice around the globe and, in contrast, how fickle we in the West can be in our approach to these issues.

Have copies of the *Guardian* newspaper ready, ideally from several different days and including a weekend edition.

Split the group into teams of three. Give each team one or two newspapers and instruct them to spend 5 minutes searching for stories dealing with Third World nations, or poverty and injustice. They should discuss among themselves what, if anything, draws them into the story – the headline, the picture, the person interviewed, the way it's written.

Allow each team to feed back. Note their reasons for being drawn into a story. Did any find the story itself engaging, or was it the way it was presented, the headlines and the pictures that got them drawn in?

PLAY THE TRACK > > > > >

When the track has finished read out the second verse which starts, 'People going hungry . . . '

Explain that the media is always looking for an event, a reaction, an emotion and some immediacy. The track puts it bluntly. It suggests that the death of a child is what makes interesting TV and what provides food for a hungry public.

Ask the following questions. Allow each person to have their say:

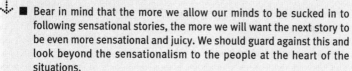

- The only things we see on our screen are the sensational things. News by definition has to have a current and slightly sensational hook on it to make it to the screens or into the newspaper columns. True or false?

- The media jumps out of covering stories as quickly as it jumps into covering them. As soon as the stories go off the boil, they go off the news agenda. True or false?

Suggest the following action, which young people can take to get beyond what the media tells them:

- Watch the stories of this nature that come up on the news. Record how many days they are covered in the press or TV to get an idea of how quickly the media lens leaves a situation.

- Link up with relief and development agencies. Try www.tearfund.org or www.christian-aid.org.uk for starters. Order their free (youth) magazines and prayer guides.

- Bear in mind that the more we allow our minds to be sucked in to following sensational stories, the more we will want the next story to be even more sensational and juicy. We should guard against this and look beyond the sensationalism to the people at the heart of the situations.

Sum up by challenging the group to get into pairs and together begin to take a long-term interest in one or two specific global situations. Suggest they contact Tearfund and Christian Aid and search the web for information.

End by reading Psalm 94.

33. JESUS' BLOOD

TRACK 14: Jesus' Blood

LENGTH: 5 mins 55 secs

IN BRIEF: A chance to look at what the death of Jesus and the spilling of his blood meant for us.

Album:
Glo
(Furious, 2000)

Artist:
Delirious?

APPLICATION

Using the following, build a picture for the group of the story of Christianity and how and where the blood of Jesus fits into it. This should help prevent the crucifixion being seen as an isolated event and provide some background on what led God to send Jesus.

> For 1,400 years before Jesus came, God had been trying to keep his people, Israel, looking to him. He sent messengers – prophets – to give guidance, but the people kept getting distracted by what was around them. They would often repent and sacrifice an animal to fulfil God's law and receive forgiveness when the animal's blood was spilt.
>
> However, over time God's people forgot, or deliberately ignored him.
>
> The people never fully turned back to God and nearly 600 years before Jesus came, around 2,600 years ago, God's holy city of Jerusalem was invaded and destroyed. The temple, which signified God's presence with his people, was demolished. Had God run out of patience?
>
> No, he had decided that a new strategy was needed. He would go to the people himself in the person of Jesus.
>
> Throughout the Old Testament, the spilling of the blood of an animal was used for the forgiveness of sin. In the New Testament is was Jesus' blood that would be spilt.

Encourage the group to think about the idea of friendship as they listen to the track.

PLAY THE TRACK > > > > >

Within the first 33 seconds of the music, before the singing starts, read out the following: *'Jesus said, "The greatest love a person can show is to die for his friends"'* (John 15:13).

At 3 minutes 25 seconds, the music changes tone and the sound of Jesus being nailed to the cross is heard. If you can, prior to the meeting, get (or make) a simple cross as a visual aid and have it standing upright. Have a hammer and some fairly large nails by the cross. Over the sound of the nails being banged in on the track, say:

> *Jesus was nailed to a real cross with real nails. He felt real pain. He gritted his teeth and stuck it out. He accepted the pain because he knew that if he didn't we wouldn't have a chance. Jesus demonstrated his level of friendship and love. We didn't know who he was, but he knows us and suffered because he wanted us to know him.*

The song ends at 5 minutes 55 seconds. However, it carries on for another 5 minutes into track 15. Allow the music to run on and ask one person (who you have primed prior to the meeting) to read a section of the crucifixion story: John 19:1-22.

Depending on the way your church operates, this may be a good opportunity to celebrate Christ's death with communion. If so, lead into this with prayer. If that is not appropriate, encourage the group to reflect on Jesus' friendship towards us using these questions:

- Jesus showed he loved people when they were either unaware of, or ignoring, him. How does Jesus' friendship affect how we live our lives?

- The track refers to Jesus as 'king, friend and saviour'. How do you see Jesus? Why do you think you see him in this way?

- What does 'laying down our lives for our friends' mean today?

- The track says, 'Jesus' blood never fails me'. What does that mean? Is this your experience?

If there is time, end by getting the group to create a mural around the line, 'Jesus' blood never fails me' on a sheet or roll of wallpaper. They should write/spray the words in the centre and around them depict with words and drawings what this means for them in their lives.

34. OLD FOR NEW

TRACK 7: My Glorious

LENGTH: 6 mins 10 secs

IN BRIEF: A chance for the group to consider how God is changing the old for the new in them.

Album:
Glo
(Furious, 2000)

Artist:
Delirious?

APPLICATION

Before the group arrive have the following line from the song displayed on a wall, either sprayed on a sheet or written in marker pen on some large paper: **'All You Ever Do is Change the Old for New'**.

Split the group into two teams. Explain that you will ask a question and the first team to shout 'Yes' gets the opportunity to answer the question. All the questions relate to someone or something being changed into something new:

1. What animal enters a cocoon and comes out looking totally different? (*caterpillar*)

2. Which well-known Apostle did God change the name of on the Damascus road? (*Paul – formerly Saul*)

3. In winter, what does water become when it freezes? (*ice*)

4. What changed Pharaoh's mind about letting the people of Israel go? (*the Plagues*)

5. What causes the tides to change? (*the moon*)

6. In cooking, what liquid is butter made from? (*milk*)

7. In the Old Testament, God changes Abram's name to what? (*Abraham*)

Tell the group that all of these questions relate to someone or something experiencing a change into something new – Paul to Saul; a caterpillar to a butterfly; milk to butter etc. The track they are about to hear deals with God making us into new people.

PLAY THE TRACK > > > > >

Raise these questions, allowing 5 minutes for people to think about each answer in their own heads:

- The song says 'all you ever do is change the old for new'. God keeps changing elements of our old lives for new ones. Do you ever feel like you've messed up once too often?

- What does it mean in your life that 'God is bigger than the air I breathe'? What situations do you need God to show you that he is bigger than at the moment?

- The song refers to clouds breaking and a down-pouring of heaven on earth. Where do you see evidence of that in your life and around you?

Close by playing the track again and inviting the group, as it plays, to talk to God about anything that has come up out of the questions.

PLAY THE TRACK AGAIN > > > > >

God keeps changing elements of our old lives for new ones

35. CONNECTED TO GOD

TRACKS 11, 12, 13 (CD 2): If We'd Ask

LENGTH: 7 mins 7 secs in total

IN BRIEF: An opportunity for the group to meet with God and hear him speak through everyday objects.

Album:
Access:D
(Furious, 2002)

Artist:
Delirious?

APPLICATION

These tracks are about asking God to come and meet us. The fact that it's a live recording adds to the atmosphere. Treat the three songs as one whole track, allowing them to flow into each other.

Start by reading 1 Corinthians 14:26 and Ephesians 4:11-13 from a modern translation.

Ask this question: When we meet together as a group to connect with God, is it just between us and God, or between us, God and others?

Tell the group: We are going to ask God to come and meet with us. In the Bible God comes to his people to equip them to help them worship him and to make them more effective tools in the world. The verse we read out makes the point that when Christians gather to meet God they should keep each other in mind and think about strengthening the whole group, not just themselves.

Read Matthew 7:7-11 and encourage the group to relax and, if they feel comfortable, to keep their eyes open so that meeting with God is a whole group experience.

PLAY THE TRACK > > > > >

At 1 minute 5 seconds into track 12 (2 minutes 50 seconds from the start of track 11), ask the group to follow the singer's instructions to hold hands as a symbol of breaking down barriers of age, colour and sex.

At 2 minutes 20 into track 12 (4 minutes 5 seconds from the start of track 11), invite the group to pray for God's blessing on other members of the group. Either suggest that they pray for the person on their right or leave the group to find people on their own. Print out the blessing Moses spoke over Israel in Numbers 7:24-26 and give a copy to each person prior to the meeting to use as a guide of what to pray.

As the track finishes, ask for feedback on who felt that they met with God. What did it feel like? Make the point that sometimes God is ever present and waiting to say things to us through everyday things around us.

Have some water (in a glass) ready to place on view along with sand, earth and some leaves from trees. Also give out paper and pens.

Explain that Christians believe God created nature. He is not in nature, but his fingerprints are. Nature therefore reflects something of God. Look at the water, sand, earth and leaves in front of you. Study them for a few minutes and identify any clues these give of God. What purpose does the earth serve? What is the texture of sand? How does it feel to float in water – and what does this tell us about God's presence?

After giving them 10 minutes to write down their thoughts, give out hand mirrors to each member of the group – or one between two if numbers are restricted. Explain that in Genesis 1:27 it says that God created male and female in his image. We reflect things about God. Think about that for a moment. Your body, your mind, your hands, your thoughts, all reflect something about your creator – God.

When Christians gather to meet God they should keep each other in mind

Instruct them to select a part of their body – arm, hand, finger, foot, head, face, whatever and to spend 5 minutes thinking deeply about what that part of their body says about God.

Ask them to share their insights and then close with a prayer time.

Encourage the group to be reminded of God's imprint on them through the week as they look at the part of their body they have studied. Encourage them to use this as a stimulus to meeting with God.

36. TRANSPARENT

TRACK 14 (CD 2): Investigate

LENGTH: 8 mins 12 secs

IN BRIEF: This session helps young people open up their inner selves to God.

Album:
Access:D
(Furious, 2002)

Artist:
Delirious?

APPLICATION

Start by making the point that we often see being interviewed or investigated in a negative or intrusive way. However, if we have a medical examination, though it may be painful or intrusive, we are the ones who benefit in the long run.

ASK:

- When someone interviews, investigates or examines you, what are they trying to find out?
- Is it possible in these situations to mislead the person asking the questions?

Ask one of the group to read out Jeremiah 17:10, then ask:

- Do we need to give God permission to search our hearts?
- Do you feel glad or scared hearing that verse read?

Depending on responses to the last question, encourage them that the Bible sees every day as a new day and that God always deals with us in love. Say that Christ chose to die for us knowing our sin – it's not a shock to him.

Give out photocopies of a window you have drawn on a blank sheet of paper with a curtain rail above it, but no curtains. Above the window, mark the words **'Window Into My Life'**. When each person has a sheet and pen, say to them that as you play the track you want them to be very honest with themselves. Tell them it's just between them and God, and you want them to draw curtains on the window to reflect how much they want God to investigate their lives. If they want God to see it all, draw the curtains wide open.

PLAY THE TRACK > > > > >

Instruct them to draw the curtains as it plays.

Spend 10 minutes praying with a difference. Allow the group to respond to God in whatever way they feel comfortable. Have paints, brushes and paper, clay, Bibles and any other things you know your group might work well with as aids to prayer. Encourage them to use their creations as prayers to God relating to him investigating their lives. Have some music playing in the background while this happens.

PLAY THE TRACK AGAIN > > > > >

Give out a similar sheet with the window on, but this time with the words of Psalm 139:23 written in the window so that if they draw the curtains part-shut they will obscure the words. Tell them to use this as their prayer to God, whether it's a 'come and investigate me' prayer or a 'help me to be ready for you to search me' prayer.

End by giving out Psalm 17:3 as a verse to inspire them to live right in the week ahead.

'Search me, O God, and know my heart; test me and know my anxious thoughts'.

37. MAKING A DIFFERENCE

TRACK 6: Thankyou

LENGTH: 3 mins 38 secs

IN BRIEF: A chance to reflect on the power we have to brighten or destroy others' lives.

Album:
No Angel
(BMG, 2000)

Artist:
Dido

APPLICATION

Turn up to the meeting with a very serious expression on your face as if you are in a bad mood. The session will show how each member of the group can affect someone else's day, making it bright or unhappy. Prior to the meeting, arrange with a member of the group that you will have an argument with them about something they say which grates on you. Script the argument in your heads so that it looks authentic. Don't let on to the others that any of this is part of the meeting or has been planned.

After the argument, come clean and ask how it made those who overheard the dispute feel. Unhappy? Disappointed? Sad? Ask your acting partner whether they felt uneasy, even though they knew you were not really having a go at them.

Explain that in this meeting you are going to be looking at the power within each one of us to brighten up, or to destroy, other people's lives.

Ask around the room for stories of the best day of people's lives, and what made it so special. Most stories will involve other people. Very few people will say their best day was spent on their own.

Draw out this fact and point out that people are what make the difference between a dark and a bright day.

PLAY THE TRACK > > > > >

Play the track, asking the group to imagine the changes in emotions taking place as the story in the song progresses. Get feedback on this before moving on.

Have a beautiful image of nature – a mountain scene, a river – on view. You'll get these from an issue of National Geographic magazine. Ask the group to look at it while they listen to the following reading. Ask a volunteer to read this out, in a sombre tone:

> *'Life can be very, very hard. Some days I don't feel I have what it takes to get out of bed and face the world again. The view out of my bedroom is beautiful. But when I look at* [insert details here which relate to the image you have selected] *I feel sad, unhappy, depressed. I'm stuck in this village with two grannies and a goat. There's not one person within 20 years of my age. I don't relate to or feel understood by anyone round here.'*

Then invite everyone to look at a different picture. Make this one something dull – a cloudy, overcast sky. Instruct them to look at the image while another volunteer reads the following. Get them to read in an upbeat way.

> *'The fact that the weather today was as dark as the night sky and it rained enough to fill a small ocean made no difference. In fact, it made meeting up with friends I hadn't seen for two years all the more of an adventure. We ate, talked, reminisced, got wet, laughed and shopped. It was one of those days when even if the sky had fallen in, we'd have laughed at it.'*

Split the group into two. Give Luke 4:14-21 to one group with these questions:

1. Summarise the mission of Jesus from verses 18 and 19.
2. From what you know of Jesus' ministry, what do you think 'proclaiming the year of the Lord's favour' means?

To the second group give Luke 10:30-37 with these questions:

1. What do you think is the central message of this parable?
2. How would the priest and Levite have made the robbed man feel by their actions?
3. Was this costly for the Samaritan?

After each group has fed back their conclusions, produce the two images of nature used earlier. Ask:

- What sort of emotions do these images now evoke?
- What determines how you feel about these images?
- What made your memory of the best day of your life so special? The people or the surroundings?

End by playing the track again and drawing together what the group has learnt about the difference they can make to someone's life this week. Encourage them to think of one thing they can do this week to brighten up someone's day.

PLAY THE TRACK AGAIN > > > > >

38. FAITHFULNESS IN MARRIAGE

TRACK 3: Don't Think of Me

LENGTH: 4 mins 30 secs

IN BRIEF: An opportunity to look at why God takes faithfulness in marriage so seriously.

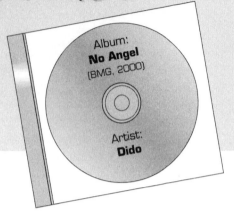

Album:
No Angel
(BMG, 2000)

Artist:
Dido

APPLICATION

This track raises the subject of when someone in a relationship is disloyal to their partner. You can gear what you say towards disloyalty in marital relationships – though the song may not relate just to married couples.

PLAY THE TRACK > > > > >

Play the track and, if appropriate, open up the floor for people to talk about their own views and understanding of adultery and extramarital affairs.

Explain that in the Bible someone who commits adultery is pictured like someone who pours red-hot coals into their own laps, and that during this session you are going to look at what the Bible teaches about loyalty in marriage.

Start by asking volunteers to read out the following verses:

Hebrews 13:4
Proverbs 2:12-19
Proverbs 5

---> ---> ---> --->

Draw out the following points:

- ■ God takes the vows people make in marriage seriously (Hebrews 13:4).

- ■ Adulterers can never be trusted. They leave their own partners and don't take commitment seriously (Proverbs 2:17).

- ■ Discipline is required to resist temptation (Proverbs 5:12 and 23).

- ■ God sees everything (Proverbs 5:21).

Ask for the group's comments on why they think God takes it so seriously. Throw in the idea that our relationship with God is built on loyalty. God is jealous (Exodus 20:5) so if we cannot stick to our vows with an earthly partner, can we stick to them with God?

Read out Ephesians 5:25-28 and draw out the parallel God makes between human marriage and his relationship to the church, his people. Emphasise that God takes his commitment to the church very seriously. By the same token, he expects people to take their marriage vows seriously.

End by having a debate. Use these questions to stimulate thinking and discussion:

- ■ Does the seriousness with which God takes marriage vows scare you?

- ■ How do you think God feels seeing so many people take their vows lightly?

- ■ Imagine you are married. How might the patterns of conduct established in your relationship before you were engaged affect your marital relationship?

Does the seriousness with which God takes marriage vows scare you?

39. WORRY

TRACK 1: Donny X

LENGTH: 4 mins 7 secs

IN BRIEF: This session looks at worry and anxiety and suggests some practical ways to deal with them.

Album:
Outrospective
(BMG, 2001)

Artist:
Faithless

APPLICATION

Ask the group to get comfortable. You may want to dim the lights, or use candles to create a more reflective, chilled atmosphere. Introduce the track by saying that worry affects us all. It can cloud our relationship with God and cause us to look in the wrong places for peace and fulfilment.

PLAY THE TRACK > > > > >

During the first 3 minutes of music read (slowly) the following scripture from Matthew 6:25-27 from *The Message* paraphrase:

> 'Steep your life in God-reality, God-initiative, God-provisions. Don't worry about missing out. You'll find all your everyday human concerns will be met. Give your entire attention to what God is doing right now and don't get worked up about what may or may not happen tomorrow. God will help you deal with whatever [tough] things come up.'

THE MESSAGE. Copyright © 1993, NavPress Publishing Group

At 3 minutes 35, the following words are heard: 'Quiet. Still. You feel there's nothing going on until you realise the space behind your eyes is filling up with something like peace. Your thoughts cease, pleasure grows in your soul. Words of comfort, strength.'

At that point, tell the group that Jesus said we shouldn't let our hearts be troubled, but should trust in God (John 14:1). This is easier said than done. It's important to recognise the part our environment (where we are, what we are listening to, looking at, thinking about) plays in determining whether we are able to really connect with God and hand over our worries to him.

Jesus said we shouldn't let our hearts be troubled, but should trust in God

PLAY THE TRACK AGAIN > > > > >

Play the track a second time. Ask people to picture in their minds any situations worrying them right now. As they listen to the music, encourage them to picture themselves handing those situations to Jesus. Tell them to think on his promise in Matthew: 'God will help you deal with whatever [tough] things come up.'

Ask people if they use music as an aid to meeting with God and handing worries over to him. Encourage them to see their favourite tracks or albums as tools to help them to do this. Ask them to tell the group which music they use for this.

Brainstorm practical steps to overcoming worry. Use these ideas to get the group started:

- Is it irrational? Decide whether the worry has become bigger in your mind than it should be. If it has, talk to someone about it and get their perspective to help bring it back down to size.

- Are you avoiding someone, somewhere or something on account of the worry? If so, it may be time to face up to them.

- Have you prayed with someone about the thing that's worrying you? If not, find a friend and ask for prayer.

- Have you read the Bible and looked at how Jesus dealt with things that worried him?

Conclude by asking who is worrying about something that feels too big to overcome? Make the point that Jesus said trusting in him was an alternative to worry. Brainstorm what this might mean in practice this week.

MUSIC TO MOVE THE SOUL 39

40. WHAT'S AT THE CENTRE?

TRACK 12: Liontamer

LENGTH: 5 mins 45 secs

IN BRIEF: A chance to look at why putting Jesus at the centre of your life, in front of other attractions, is so important.

Album:
Outrospective
(BMG, 2001)

Artist:
Faithless

APPLICATION

The track starts with the lyrics: 'If you place a thing at the centre of your life that lacks the power to nourish, it will eventually poison everything that you are and destroy you.' Read out this line, explaining that it is from the track they will hear later. Give out paper and pens and tell the group to get into pairs. Each pair then has 5 minutes to talk about and make a list of the things that are close to the centre of their lives. Suggest that the following points are a good test for whether something is close to their hearts:

- If you think about it regularly.
- If you look forward to seeing/using it.
- If you would find it hard to part with it.
- If you spend money on it.

Come back together as a group and get people to shout out some of the things they wrote down. Invite them, as they listen to the song, to think about the lyrics in relation to the things on their list.

PLAY THE TRACK > > > > >

Now ask them how Jesus fares on the four-point test (above). Encourage them to be honest. Discuss their answers.

Do an exercise looking at why Jesus seemed to emphasise to people who wanted to be his disciples that they must put him, and not other attractions, at the centre of their lives. Split the group into two and give one of the following sets of verses to each group.

GROUP 1: Matthew 10:34-39; Luke 12:32-34

GROUP 2: Matthew 6:19-21; Matthew 6:24

They should consider these questions as they read them:

- What do these verses say that Jesus must be above in our lives?
- What do these verses say about the reward for putting Jesus at the centre?
- How central are these things in your life?

Read out Matthew 6:21, then tell the group that the Bible says that our hearts will follow and treasure the things we put great value on – the things we spend most time thinking about, spending money on or engaging in.

Come back together. Let the groups feed back and then tell them that, 35 seconds into the track, the lyrics read: 'No one can be the source of your content, it lies within, at the centre'. Read out John 4:14 and explain that it is only when we allow Jesus to have the central place in our lives that he can bring real satisfaction.

It is only when we allow Jesus to have the central place in our lives that he can bring real satisfaction

41. CHURCH

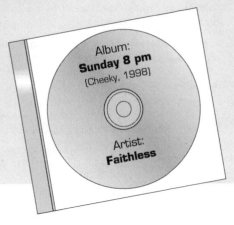

TRACK 8: God is a DJ

LENGTH: 8 mins

IN BRIEF: This session helps young people unpack and think through what church really is.

Album:
Sunday 8 pm
(Cheeky, 1998)

Artist:
Faithless

APPLICATION

Start by giving everyone a pen and sheet of paper. Ask them to shut their eyes and imagine that they have been visited by the angel of the Lord and given a commission to come up with a plan for a twenty-first-century church. With their eyes still shut, tell them that the only condition given by the angel was that the guiding principle for the church must be to help people grow in their knowledge of God and become more like Jesus.

After a few minutes invite them to open their eyes and jot down any ideas they had.

Have several piles of magazines, scissors and glue at the ready. Divide the group into small teams and give them 5 minutes to create as many misfits of heads onto bodies, using pictures cut from the magazines, as they can.

Put those to one side and tell the group that the track they are about to hear introduces the subject of church in today's culture.

PLAY THE TRACK > > > > >

When the track has finished ask who likes the idea of a nightclub being their church and of God being the DJ? Who struggles with that concept? Why?

Invite people to feed back any ideas they had earlier for making a twenty-first-century church. Follow this by working as one big group to come up with an 'essentials' list of things that are vital to any church. You might want to read Ephesians 4:11-16 to introduce the idea of the church as a body. Ensure the list includes the following:

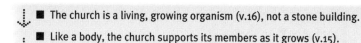

- The church is a living, growing organism (v.16), not a stone building.
- Like a body, the church supports its members as it grows (v.15).
- The prime function of the church is to grow as a body towards its head, Christ (v.15).
- Diversity is important. Each person has different roles to fulfil (v.16) and gifts to bring.

Play the following game to illustrate the need to be aware of the guidelines and markers for any journey before you start out. Lay a winding course from one end of the room to the other using beakers as markers. Pick several volunteers and show them the course they must walk. Blindfold them and spin them several times to disorientate them. Invite them to walk the course you have marked.

When this is finished, make the point that this can be like church in modern culture: we can easily lose our way if we don't keep our eyes on the essentials of what church is about.

Go through the 'essentials' list you came up with earlier and ask the following:

- What is absent from the list? (Specifics e.g. style of music.)
- What is present in the list? (The skeleton principles on which each generation can hang their specific preferences.)

Explain that the principles of what church really is deal with the objectives, mission and direction of a church, not with how these are worked out for each generation. Paul wrote about the principle of growing together in Christ, but didn't specify how that should be done. Each generation will use different vehicles for essentials such as worship (hymn books, song books, guitars, record decks), supporting its members (prayer triplets, home groups, residentials) and growing in Christ (Bible studies, sermons, 24-7 prayer rooms).

PLAY THE TRACK AGAIN > > > > >

Tell the group to try to look beyond the specifics (buildings, structures, styles of worship) and try to see how the principles of church can fit into the idea of church put forward in this track.

End by using the misfits they cut out earlier to provide a broad picture of what church is about: being prepared as a body of God's people for Christ – the Head – to return.

42. EDEN

TRACK 1: The Garden

LENGTH: 4 mins 27 secs

IN BRIEF: This session brings the story of Eden to life and looks at humanity's thirst for knowledge and answers.

Album:
Sunday 8 pm
(Cheeky, 1998)

Artist:
Faithless

APPLICATION

The byline for this track is 'even sitting in the garden one can still get stung'.

There are no lyrics, but the music is like a journey, progressing to higher intensity as it goes and providing an evocative soundtrack. Use it to powerful effect as backing sound for a reading of the story of Adam and Eve in Eden.

To get the best out of this, ensure everyone is comfortable. Invite the group to shut their eyes and let their imaginations bring to life the account they will hear read.

Leave a minute's silence and then read Genesis 2:4-9.

PLAY THE TRACK > > > > >

Read the following sections to fit in with the timings of the track. It's a good idea to rehearse before doing it with a group.

 0-80 seconds: Genesis 1:27-31

 84-120 seconds: Genesis 3:1-6

120-267 seconds: Genesis 3:7-15 and Genesis 3:23-24

After the track has finished, **EITHER**:

PLAY THE TRACK AGAIN > > > > >

Play the track again and read the following meditation:

> *God took seven days to make the world.*
>
> *Human beings were the cherry on the cake of his creation.*
>
> *In his image, in his likeness he made them.*
>
> *God withheld nothing from his creation – the animals, plants, trees and birds were put under Adam and Eve's care.*
>
> *One thing he kept back. One small tree, in a garden bursting with beautiful flowers, trees, fruits, green plants and clear rivers.*
>
> *But humanity struggled to be content with not knowing everything.*
>
> *Seeking greater wisdom and knowledge, Adam and Eve bit the fruit.*
>
> *Thousands of years later, we struggle with the same thing: not knowing all the answers, we demand that God give us insight into his mysteries.*
>
> *We demand knowledge. We lack faith to believe God knows best.*
>
> *The lesson of Eden is to find contentment in what God has given, and not to explore discontentment with what he hasn't.*

OR

Get a discussion going using these questions:

- Whose fault was the expulsion from Eden?
- Why did God throw Adam and Eve out of Eden? (Genesis 3:22)
- Why do you think God pronounced punishments? (Genesis 3:16-19)
- What does this account say about human ability to be content or to need to know everything?

OR

PLAY THE TRACK AGAIN > > > > >

Play the track again and have a prayer time, thanking God for the energy he put into making our environment sweet. Thank him that even when Adam and Eve had sinned, he still came close to them and made clothes for them.

43. WAYS TO PRAISE

TRACK 9: Praise You

LENGTH: 5 mins 22 secs

IN BRIEF: To look at what it means to praise God. To think of different ways to praise him and to examine the way King David praised God.

Album:
You've Come A Long Way Baby
(Skint, 1998)

Artist:
Fatboy Slim

APPLICATION

Start with a quiz. Divide the group into several smaller teams. Give them 5 minutes to come up with as many Christian praise songs as they can. Award a prize for whichever team thinks of the most songs.

Have an empty cardboard box in the centre of the room. When the quiz is finished, ask each team to put their song lists in the box.

PLAY THE TRACK > > > > >

Place a piece of paper saying **'Yes'** at one end of the room, one saying **'Maybe'** in the centre and one saying **'No'** at the opposite end. Ask these questions and suggest the group indicates their thoughts by standing near the appropriate sheet of paper. Be sure to ask some of them why they think that each time. Ask the following questions:

Can you praise God when

- you are smoking?
- you are at school?
- you are in a nightclub?
- you have just argued with your parents?

Do you often praise God when

- you are ill?
- you are happy?
- you are on holiday?
- you are desperate?
- you are sad?

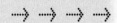

Brainstorm the question 'What does it mean to praise God?' then give each person a blank sheet of paper and a pen.

Explain that praising God is about what's in our heart not about the style we do it in. We don't always think 'outside of the box' when we plan worship or praise sessions – we stick to what we know.

Give each person 5 minutes to come up with one idea for a way of praising God that is 'outside the box'. Ask them to write the idea on their sheet of paper, be creative and think about what they enjoy doing and the style of music they enjoy listening to. Explore the idea of worship and praise using all the senses. Play the track again while they do this.

After 5 minutes, go round the room and allow each person to present their idea and explain how they came up with it. As each person does this, they should lay the sheet of paper with the idea on it around the outside of the box. Make the connection that these ideas are 'outside the box' ideas.

Move on to a Bible study, looking at King David and how he praised God.

Explain that the Ark of the Lord was a symbol of God's presence with Israel. For King David, bringing it to Jerusalem was a sign of God's presence with them. Ask a volunteer to read 2 Samuel 6:16-23 and discuss the significance of this account for us today:

- What does David's exuberant worship say about who he was more concerned about – God or the onlookers? Who are we more concerned about?

- Was God pleased with David's act of praise (see 2 Samuel 7:1-3)? Which elements of our worship today do you think please God?

- What was at the root of Michal's concern over David's expression of praise (2 Samuel 6:20)? How could she have dealt with her problem?

Close with a time of prayer. Encourage the group to keep to praise prayers for what God has done.

Praising God is about what's in our heart not about the style we do it in

44. GUIDANCE

Album:
You've Come A Long Way Baby
(Skint, 1998)

Artist:
Fatboy Slim

TRACK 10: Love Island

LENGTH: 5 mins 18 secs

IN BRIEF: A look at how God guides us, and what to do when you are in the dark about the future.

APPLICATION

This upbeat dance track makes great backing sound for this session.

PLAY THE TRACK > > > > >

ASK:

'Who has ever come to a crossroads in their life and had no idea which way they should go?' Give opportunity for anyone who wants to share to talk about their experiences of guidance.

Explain the basics of biblical guidance to the group, using the following:

■ WHO: God guides us. When we are in danger of going the wrong way, he always steps in. Read Isaiah 30:21 to illustrate this point.

■ WHAT: We can seek God's guidance on anything. God's arm is not too short.

■ WHERE: We can seek God's guidance anywhere. Psalm 139:9-10 says that even if we settle on the far side of the sea God is there.

■ WHEN: The best way to see God's hand guiding you is after the event. Looking back you can see evidence of God guiding you.

■ WHY: We seek God's guidance because he is above everything and sees the end from the beginning. He uses this knowledge to guide us.

■ HOW: In the Old Testament, God guided by means of a cloud over his people. Today, God guides through his Holy Spirit. Read John 16:13.

If the track has finished, set it to 'repeat' on the CD player and let it continue playing.

Send two people out of the room. Lay out four eggs in a path across the room (lay plastic down if you don't want broken eggs on the floor). Instruct some of those still in the room to shout the wrong directions to the person when they return blindfolded to try and walk the path, so that they step on the eggs and others to call out the right instructions.

Bring in one of the people and tell them they have to walk the narrow path from one end of the room to the other without breaking the eggs. They must walk the path blindfolded, but let them see the eggs before you blindfold them.

Repeat the exercise with the second person. Then do the same exercise all over again but this time allocate a guide to the blindfolded volunteers to hold their arm and lead them so that they can walk without breaking the eggs.

Sum up by making these points:

- When we try and walk into the unknown without God guiding us, we listen to the wrong voices and end up going the wrong way.
- When we allow God to lead us, he has the benefit of not being in the dark about what's ahead.

End by splitting the group into smaller clusters and inviting them to pray for each other concerning anything that they are uncertain about or for which they need God's guidance.

Give out slips of paper with Isaiah 30:21 printed on for them to take away.

When we are in danger of going the wrong way, God always steps in

45. GLOBAL EMERGENCIES

TRACK 6: Emergency on Planet Earth

LENGTH: 4 mins 4 secs

IN BRIEF: A chance to look at racism, hunger and poverty and think about our role in bringing change.

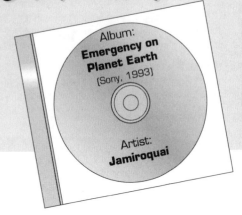

Album:
Emergency on Planet Earth
(Sony, 1993)

Artist:
Jamiroquai

APPLICATION

PLAY THE TRACK > > > > >

Play the track and ask the group to listen out for some of the emergencies Jay K sings about. You may want to read the lyrics of the song from the CD inlay when it has finished to help the group identify some of these.

Tell the group that you are going to look at three of the issues raised in the song: racism, hunger and poverty. Have an open discussion in which you invite members of the group to share their own experiences of these issues.

Divide the group into smaller clusters and give each several recent newspapers. Give them 10 minutes to find any stories that cover any of the themes of racism, hunger and poverty. They should read the stories in their clusters and then when the group comes back together, present what they found.

Have a globe or wall map of the world stuck up. After each group has presented their stories ask them to stick the story to the country it relates to.

You may wish to prepare by visiting the Tearfund (www.tearfund.org) or Christian Aid (www.christian-aid.org.uk) websites and print off stories or statistics relating to these issues.

Tell the group that issues of hunger, poverty and equality have always been close to God's heart. They have a lot to do with justice, and in the Old Testament many of God's prophets brought messages about these issues.

Make sure that everyone has a Bible with them and ask volunteers to read the following verses relating to the themes raised in the song:

> **RACISM** – Ezekiel 22:29
> **HUNGER** – Isaiah 58:6-7
> **POVERTY** – Amos 5:11-15

Also ask volunteers to read the following verses about God's desire for justice and ask:

Isaiah 59:11-16	What was God looking for (v.16a)?
Micah 6:8	What does this mean for us today?
Zechariah 7:9-10	What is God's call to his true followers?

Explain that God is looking to us to fight for justice in the areas of racism, hunger and poverty. We might think these issues are restricted to overseas, but they are not. There is hunger, poverty and racism in the UK as well. Re-read Isaiah 59:16 emphasising the role they have to play.

Ask the group to brainstorm where they think these things exist in the UK and in their own town. What do they think they can do about these issues? Write down their ideas and add these to the list:

■ Contact Tearfund or another charity and sign up for one of their summer trips in the UK to work in an area of great need. Individuals or whole youth groups can sign up.

■ Volunteer at a local soup kitchen for the homeless and hungry.

■ Be aware of your own stereotypes and attitudes in these areas and align your attitudes with God's.

PLAY THE TRACK AGAIN > > > > >

Read out some of the verses used above. Invite the group to imagine any action they take as being like a stone thrown in a still lake – the effects bring about change and the ripples move out far beyond where the stone entered.

46. TOO YOUNG TO DIE?

TRACK 2: Too Young To Die

LENGTH: 6 mins 4 secs

IN BRIEF: A look at how long we might live, what the Bible says about our allotted days and what it's like to grow older.

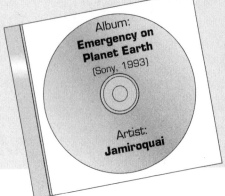

Album:
Emergency on Planet Earth
(Sony, 1993)

Artist:
Jamiroquai

APPLICATION

Start by reading Psalm 139:16 and introducing the idea that the length of time we live is determined by God.

Do the following quiz. The group should put their hands up if they think the statement is true and lower it if they think it's false:

1. Methuselah was Noah's grandfather and he lived to 969 years of age. He had a son when he was aged 187. *(true)*

2. Methuselah's father didn't die – the Bible says God 'took him away'. *(true – Genesis 5:24)*

3. Jesus raised Lazarus from the dead twice because he fell into a pit and died a second time three months after Jesus first raised him. *(false)*

4. The prophet Elijah didn't die – he was taken to heaven in a whirlwind and a chariot of fire. *(true)*

5. Mary the mother of Jesus lived to the ripe old age of 147. *(false)*

6. When Joseph died, he was embalmed (preserved from decay). *(true – Genesis 50:26)*

7. Judas, the disciple, killed himself by swallowing acid from a poisonous tree. *(false)*

8. Peter, the disciple, died by being crucified upside down. *(true – according to legend)*

PLAY THE TRACK > > > > >

Go around the group and ask what age people think they will live to. Then ask them to shout out the age after which they would not feel they were too young to die. Then ask these questions:

- What is it that makes you think you have to live to be a certain age? (In some countries 45 is the average life span.)

- When you are 65, how do you think you will be different to how you are now in both attitude and dress?

Prior to the session, ask several of the group to video some vox pops of older people talking about what it is like getting older, how what they want from life has changed as they have grown older, and whether they think they will ever be ready to die.

Show the vox pops at this point.

Divide the group into four smaller clusters. Set up a hot seat and explain that each team has to field one or two people (depending on numbers and time) to put the case to God as to why they should be allowed to live to the age that they would like to live to. The three other teams must give marks out of 10 for how convincing each person is. Once all the teams have done this, give a prize to the winning team.

Explain that the Bible is clear that how long we live is in God's control. Psalm 31:15 talks about our 'times' being in God's hands. This is an important thing for us to grasp. We must walk the line between not thinking we will live for ever and therefore never thinking about our earthly death and, on the other hand, not spending too much time worrying about when we will die.

End by reading Ecclesiastes 12:1-7 to draw together these two threads.

The Bible is clear that how long we live is in God's control

47. SPECIAL VISION

TRACK 5: Night Vision

LENGTH: 5 mins 5 secs

IN BRIEF: This session deals with the special vision God gives us when he asks something big of us.

Album:
Brooklyn & Beyond
(Survivor/Emerge, 2002)

Artist:
DJ Kenny Mitchell

APPLICATION

Before the meeting spray-paint on an old sheet the words: **'A Vision Not of Man But of Spirit. A Night Vision.'** Have this suspended for the group to see. If appropriate, you could ask, in advance, a couple of the 'arty' ones to do this for you, adding their own designs. If space doesn't permit, write this on a sheet of card or on a laptop.

Start by asking for a volunteer. Set up a chair in the middle and sit them on it. Divide the rest into two groups – one 'for' and one 'against'.

Lay this challenge before the person: You are nearly 75 years old. You think God is asking you to leave the very nice, wealthy area you have always lived in and move hundreds of miles to a poorer, run-down area. You are close to your family and you love them. But God is asking you to leave them – probably never to see them again. The 900-mile journey will involve many dangers and, ultimately, you know little of the being who has called you to do this – this is one of your first encounters with God.

The 'for' and 'against' groups then have 5 minutes each to try and persuade the person on the seat why they should/shouldn't take up the challenge. At the end, the seated candidate must choose either way and say why.

Read out Genesis 12:1-3, the call of Abraham, on which the above situation was based. Before you play the track, ask the group to think about the size of the challenge God was putting before Abraham and about what God would give to Abraham to equip him for this.

PLAY THE TRACK > > > > >

As you play the track, explain that God gave Abraham 'night vision' to help him. This enabled him to see, understand and connect with things that were happening in the spiritual realm – God's plans and ideas. Ask the group to talk about any times they felt God gave them 'night vision' – the ability to look at things from God's perspective and to trust in his deeper purpose.

1 minute 28 seconds into the track, tell them that obedience costs. Living in a way that follows God's tune, not our own or someone else's, requires us to deny what sometimes feels right and obvious. But God gives us special vision and understanding to help us. And he asks us not to be afraid

Explain that as you play the track again you will read an account of a time when Peter failed to exercise 'night vision' and Jesus had to correct him. Encourage them to think about how and when they exercise night vision.

PLAY THE TRACK AGAIN > > > > >

At around 48 seconds into it, read out Matthew 16:21-26 (from the CEV translation, if available).

Ask the group:

■ What are some practical ways you can work on developing 'night vision'? (Prayer; listening to God in normal everyday situations; asking God for help and guidance in decisions; reading scripture.)

■ Jesus said: 'If you give up your life for me, you will find it'. How do you know if you are 'holding on' to your life too much?

■ How do you 'give up' your life for Jesus?

How do you know if you are 'holding on' to your life too much?

48. GENERATIONS

TRACK 3: Next Step

LENGTH: 4 mins 44 secs

IN BRIEF: An opportunity to explore why different generations see things differently.

Album:
Brooklyn & Beyond
(Survivor/Emerge, 2002)

Artist:
DJ Kenny Mitchell

APPLICATION

Start by asking the group the following questions and getting them to shout out their answers:

- How old is the oldest person you've ever met?

- Who has ever spent time listening to an older person talk about the world they grew up in? How different did it sound to the world they now live in?

- Who sometimes finds approaches and attitudes of older people hard to understand or digest?

- Who dreads getting older? Why?

If possible, get some of the group to go out prior to the meeting and record or video an interview with an older person about how the world they grew up in is different to the world today, and about the amount and speed of change in society since they were young. They should also ask about the sort of music that was popular and social activities they did when they were the age your young people are.

When you have played the tape, say: Many of the conflicts in churches arise because of a lack of understanding between the generations.

Have a series of objects on display including: a glossy teen, fashion or culture magazine; a pair of quality trainers – affix a price tag of £70 onto these; a pot-noodle; a disposable camera, and a alco-pop drink of some kind.

Different generations have their perspectives on life formed in different times

Split the group in half. One half must imagine they are older people who experienced World War II, grew up in a time when marriage was for life, divorce was unheard of and people got on with the hard graft of life – they worked or starved. The second group should be themselves. One after the other, invite each group to look at each of the objects and shout out suggested answers to the following questions in relation to them:

■ What does this object say about culture?

■ What does this item say about the values that are accepted today?

■ What would people in 'my' generation think about this object?

Follow this by saying that different generations have their perspectives on life formed in different times. People born just before the war grew up at a time when food was short and freedom was under threat. When we relate to older people we need to remember that their perspective on life was forged at a very different time to ours. Can you identify some of the trends and values in society that have forged your perspective?

PLAY THE TRACK > > > > >

Tie together the material you have looked at and the way generations sometimes disagree and misunderstand each other in churches.

■ When conflict arises over styles and ways of being a church, what's most important to God – hearing and respecting others or winning battles?

■ How can young people bridge the misunderstanding gap and involve older church members in their new approaches, explaining why they are doing what they are doing?

Suggest the group organises an event at which they find out more about the world older people grew up in.

49. TIME TO CHANGE

TRACK 13: Everything is Everything

LENGTH: 4 mins 53 secs

IN BRIEF: A look at time and the change it brings to our lives. This session is built around a meditation which is done individually.

Album:
The Miseducation of Lauryn Hill
(Ruffhouse Records, 1998)

Artist:
Lauryn Hill

APPLICATION

Start by going around the room and asking each person to call out how they respond to change on a scale of 1 to 4, with 1 being 'I hate it and resist it' and 4 being 'I love it'.

Then ask everyone to think of a significant change they have experienced in their lives and to share this experience in the group, covering how it made them feel and how they responded.

PLAY THE TRACK > > > > >

ASK:

■ If you had a magic wand, is there something you would like to change in your life?

■ If you had a magic wand, is there something you would hate to see change in your life?

■ How do the following lines from the chorus in the track make you feel: 'After winter must come spring. Change, it comes eventually'? Is this true?

Explain to the group that you are going to spend 15 minutes looking at a meditation on the subject of time and change. Photocopy or print enough copies so that each person can have one. You will also need Bibles, pens and paper. Play the track again as they start the meditation.

Read the following meditation, based on Ecclesiastes 3:

Your Life and Time

Everything on earth has its own time and its own season.
There is a time for birth and death, for planting and reaping, for killing and healing.
There is a time for destroying and building, for crying and laughing, for weeping and dancing.
There is a time for throwing stones, and gathering stones.
There is a time for embracing and parting.
There is a time for finding and losing, for keeping and giving, for tearing and sewing, for listening and speaking.
There is also a time for love and hate, for war and peace.

Time is all around you.
Without it, nothing can happen. Everything stops.
Time allows the future to happen.
It's like a key God inserted into the world, a gift he gave.
Time, by its nature, is always moving. It cannot be still. It moves and changes everything.
Time brings change and change can be hard.

No one can understand time: Why do some people get more time to live than others? Why are there times when things go well, and times when life seems to fall apart? Why do the timings of things seem so random and without reason? Why can't humans escape the constraints of time and ageing?

Time can be a friend and an enemy.
It can be invisible, but it's usually when time is short that we become most aware of it.
When it seems endless, we forget or ignore it.

What time are you at? Are you spending a lot of time Laughing? Crying? Giving? Destroying? Building? Forgiving? Thinking? Hoping? Regretting? Mending?

There's not always an obvious reason why, but God has laid out the times and seasons for your life. He's given everything in your life a slot of time – its own amount of time. He's made time for you to laugh, give, receive, cry, build, undo, regret and mend, and ultimately to live and to die.

Turn to Ecclesiastes 3:1-8. Each of the actions mentioned involves change. As you read, insert your name and 'has' before each sentence so that each verse is personalised to you. Try to identify any things that 'jump out' which you are struggling with.

When you have read this, write down any 'time' you are in at the moment. Spend a few moments talking to God and asking for help to accept the change that being in this situation is bringing to your life.

Allow time at the end for feedback and prayer as a group.

50. ZION

TRACK 4: To Zion

LENGTH: 6 mins 9 secs

IN BRIEF: A biblical look at what Zion is, how Jesus developed the reality of Zion, and what Zion means for us.

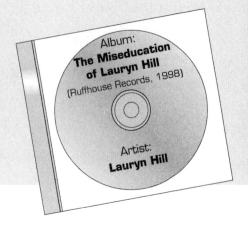

Album:
The Miseducation of Lauryn Hill
(Ruffhouse Records, 1998)

Artist:
Lauryn Hill

APPLICATION

Open the session by asking for ideas on what 'Zion' is. If ideas are short, ask for references to it in popular culture e.g. *The Matrix*, Bob Marley's music.

PLAY THE TRACK > > > > >

Ask for ideas on who, or what, the song is about. You may find some suggest the story of Mary and the birth of Jesus. If not, raise this as a possible interpretation.

Do a short Bible study on what Zion means in the Bible and how it relates to Jesus and his coming. Use the following points as a guide:

- Zion is first mentioned in the Bible as a fortress and hill near Jerusalem that King David won (2 Samuel 5:7).

- The name Zion became much more than a literal place. It came to mean the temple of God (Psalm 132:13) and eventually a word to describe God's people Israel and their land (Jeremiah 31:12. Isaiah 60:14).

- In the New Testament, the term Zion continues to evolve. It comes to relate to the spiritual Kingdom of God, which Jesus is bringing (Romans 9:33 and 11:26).

Explain that Zion came to mean the people of God in the Old Testament. In the New Testament, Jesus became the fulfilment of the kingdom of God, taking the word Zion from relating only to a select group of people (Israel) to covering everyone who is a child of God through faith.

Illustrate this by reading Luke 4:14-21. Explain that these are some of the characteristics of Zion, which Jesus turned into reality during his life. God expects us to do the same if we are children of Zion.

Refer back to the track and the chorus where the singer talks about the joy of her world being in Zion. Ask what this lyric means and what significance Zion has for us today.

Ask a volunteer to read Mary's song which she sings when she hears she is to be the mother of Jesus, in Luke 1:46-55.

End by challenging the group. Say that the track talked about having joy in Zion. Mary's song shows that her joy came from God. Zion is now a spiritual reality. It is a spiritual place, which becomes reality as we live it.

There may have been a lot to digest in this session. Allow time for questions and comments at the end.

Zion is a spiritual place, which becomes reality as we live it

51. ESCAPE

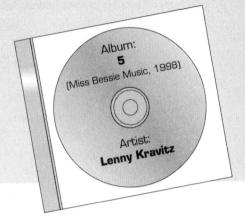

TRACK 8: Fly Away

LENGTH: 3 mins 40 secs

IN BRIEF: This session looks at the temptation to flee from difficult things and at how God can help us face these.

Album:
5
(Miss Bessie Music, 1998)

Artist:
Lenny Kravitz

APPLICATION

Introduce the theme – the temptation to sometimes throw off responsibility and fly away – by giving everyone a deflated balloon. Instruct some of them to half inflate their balloons and the rest to fully inflate them. Make sure no one ties them up.

Explain that when the pressure in our lives builds up we become like these balloons. We feel like popping and when it feels too much we wish we could just fly away.

At this point, instruct those with the fully inflated balloons to let them go.

Tell them that when we do fly off at someone or do something else to relieve the pressure, we usually end up crashing to the floor like these balloons. The alternative is to face up to our pressures and responsibilities. By doing that, we take the pressure off ourselves and reduce the risk of either exploding or flying away.

At this point, instruct those with half full balloons to release some of the air without letting them fly off.

PLAY THE TRACK > > > > >

ASK:

- Why is the idea of just flying away so tempting?

- Is flying off to laze on a beach somewhere really true freedom?

Tell the group that you are going to look at an account of one of God's prophets who 'flew away'. He couldn't face the pressure involved in what God wanted him to do, and so, like the balloon, he flew away.

Ask a volunteer to read out Jonah 1:1-3 then ask:

- Was Jonah finding freedom by running, or was he in fact escaping from freedom and being controlled by his fear?

Choose someone else to read Jonah 1:11-17 and ask:

- What Jonah was running from, kept following him. Have you ever tried to run away from the pressures you are under, only for it to feel as if they are following you?

Get a third person to read Jonah 3:1-5

- How do you think Jonah felt when he finally faced up to the task?

Divide the group into pairs. Give out torches to each pair and explain that you are going to look at shadows. Dim the lights in the room and ask those with torches to make shadows by shining the torch behind their partner's hands, head or back. While they are doing this, ask what they notice about the size of the shadows compared to the real size of the object being magnified.

Put the lights back on and tell the group that the torch is like the things we fear or the pressures in our life that we want to fly away from. When we turn our backs on them, they are magnified and the pressures facing us seem bigger than they really are. But when we face up to them, they are actually small and we can handle them easily.

Set up a large bucket half-full of water. Collect enough pebbles for one per person and tell the group you are going to end by looking at God's role in helping us face challenges. Ask everyone to sit in a circle around the bucket then read out the following:

In Exodus chapter 4 God asks Moses to speak to the King of Egypt about freeing his people.

Moses responds, 'Please, Lord, I have never been a skilled speaker . . . I speak slowly and cannot find the best words . . . Please, Lord, send someone else.'

The Lord asks Moses, 'Who made a person's mouth? . . . It is I, the Lord? Now go! I will help you speak, and will teach you what to say.'

When we run from something it gets bigger in our minds, like the shadows on the wall. When we face up to the pressures God helps us.

Moses took God at his word and began an adventure which ended in the people of Israel being freed.

Think for a moment about whether there is something in your life you want to fly away from, but know that you need to face?

Select a pebble from the pile and imagine it represents the pressure you are facing.

Place it in the water as a sign that you want God's help.

Now take it back out of the bucket as a sign that you know it's your responsibility to act.

Like Moses, God can only help you when you take the first step.

When everyone has their pebble in their hands, close with a prayer time asking God to give everyone the strength to face up and not fly away.

52. BELONGING TO GOD

TRACK 3: I belong to You

LENGTH: 4 mins 16 secs

IN BRIEF: An opportunity to consider what 'belonging to God' means.

Album:
5
(Miss Bessie Music, 1998)

Artist:
Lenny Kravitz

APPLICATION

Use this track as a song of commitment to God. The words are powerful and you may want to read sections from the CD inlay as you go.

Get everyone quiet. Light a candle in a place where everyone can see it and read the first two lines of the song before starting it on the CD player.

PLAY THE TRACK > > > > >

If possible, have the CD player on repeat so that the song loops. As its starts a second time, lower the volume slightly and read the following:

> *Paul wrote that we were called to belong to Jesus. When his life was in danger he knew that, whether he lived or died, he belonged to the Lord. He knew he belonged to Christ and that Christ belonged to him.*
>
> *How do we know we belong to Jesus? The apostle John wrote that we know because we show Christ through our actions.*

Give out the following verses on slips of paper and, with the track playing, encourage them to meditate and pray on what it means to belong to Jesus, using these verses to stimulate their prayers.

> *'Those who belong to Christ Jesus have crucified their sinful selves. They have given up their old selfish feelings and the evil things they wanted to do.'* Galatians 5:24 NCV

> *'If you belonged to the world it would love you as it loves its own. But I have chosen you out of the world, so you don't belong to it.'* John 15:19 NCV

> *'You are all people who belong to the light and to the day. We do not belong to the night or to darkness so we should not be like other people who are sleeping, but we should be awake and have self-control'.* 1 Thessalonians 5:5-6 NCV

When Paul's life was in danger he knew that, whether he lived or died, he belonged to the Lord

53. YOUR FUTURE

TRACK 5: Life's a Dream

LENGTH: 4 mins 56 secs

IN BRIEF: This session unpacks how young people see their future and ideas they have about how they want their lives to pan out. It's particularly suited to when members of the group are about to start university, or are chewing over GCSE or A-Level choices.

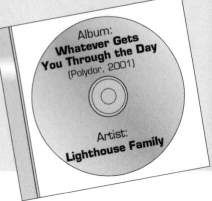

Album:
Whatever Gets You Through the Day
(Polydor, 2001)

Artist:
Lighthouse Family

APPLICATION

Start with an exercise aimed at offering young people their peers' perspective on them and on their skills and abilities. Ask everyone to write their names on separate slips of paper and place them in a bowl. Sit the group in a circle and give out a sheet of paper and pen to each person. The paper should be marked with the following categories: **'Skills'**, **'Likes'**, **'Dislikes'**, **'Dreams'**, **'Hobbies'**, **'Ideal Job'**.

Pass the bowl round asking everyone to take a name, keeping it secret. Explain that they have seven minutes to fill in any (positive) comments about the person they picked on their sheet, in the categories listed. Ensure they write the person's name on it.

Collect the sheets in and hold onto them.

Say: 'We are looking at your life and how you want to see it develop, particularly the sort of job you want to do.'

PLAY THE TRACK > > > > >

Tell them to write down the following groups of professions in the order they appeal, i.e. from most attractive to least attractive:

1. Working outdoors: 'In five years I'd like to be a gamekeeper/outdoor pursuits instructor'

2. Creative professions: 'In five years I'd like to be a builder/plasterer/landscape gardener/labourer/artist'

3. Office based: 'In five years I'd like to be a share dealer/bank manager/IT consultant/accountant.'

4. The media/communications: 'In five years I'd like to work in TV/journalism/the music industry/PR.'

5. People professions: 'In five years I would like to be a youth worker/pastor or vicar/missionary/doctor or nurse'.

Give each person the sheet from earlier. Give them 5 minutes to reflect on what is written there and on the type of jobs they picked from the list you read.

PLAY THE TRACK AGAIN > > > > >

Raise these questions/discussion starters off the back of it:

■ How important is 'knowing what you really want to do'? Why?

■ Do you find it hard to 'remember your dream' or to identify what it is you think will be the right job/career for you?

■ Is it true that fear of things going wrong stops us from trying to realise our dreams?

Draw the session together by saying: Often we don't believe in our dreams. Because they have not yet become reality, we doubt they ever will. A dream is like a window into what might be in the future. We only find out if our dream will happen when we try turning it into reality.

Have a peeled hard-boiled egg, a glass milk bottle and several matches at the ready. Place the egg so it sits in the mouth of the bottle (ensure its big enough to look like it won't fit in the bottle). With a black marker pen, write 'Dreams' on the white around the edge of the egg. Ask: 'Is this egg likely to fit inside the bottle without me pushing it or breaking it?'

Explain that our dreams about the person we want to become, jobs we want to do or ideas we want to achieve often seem like this egg – perched on the edge of becoming reality, but facing an impossible challenge as we think about making them reality.

Light the matches and drop them, lit, into the bottle. Quickly replace the egg on the mouth of the bottle and watch as it is sucked through into the bottle (a vacuum is created as the matches eat the oxygen).

End by reading Colossians 3:23 and giving that verse out on slips of paper to take away. Make the point that although this session has not examined God's role in our future employment, this principle should be our guide in whatever profession we enter.

54. CONTENTMENT

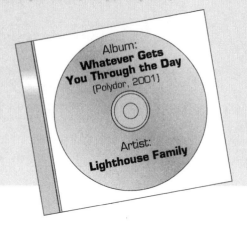

TRACK 8: You Always Want What You Haven't Got

LENGTH: 3 mins 52 secs

IN BRIEF: This session looks at how to be content with what you have.

Album:
Whatever Gets You Through the Day
(Polydor, 2001)

Artist:
Lighthouse Family

APPLICATION

Start with a dreaming session. Read out the following sentence starters and ask the group to finish them in their heads:

- If I could live in any town, city or country anywhere, I would live in . . .
- If I could wear any clothes I wanted, I would wear . . .
- If I could own any product, I would own . . .
- If I could have any job I wanted, I would be . . .
- If I could have any mobile phone I wanted, I would have . . .

Spend 5 minutes hearing their answers.

Pick several people to talk about their best memory in recent years. It could be of a holiday, a day out or an event. Note whether any of them talk about the downside of the experience.

Say that things always seem brighter in our dreams. When we think about our ideal piece of clothing or mobile, it's never the one we already have. When we look back at memories we often edit out negatives.

PLAY THE TRACK > > > > >

114

Use these points from the song as discussion starters:

- When we look over the fence, what are we missing or turning our backs on?

- Why do we 'always want what we haven't got'?

- In your experience, what determines whether you are happy or not? Is it internal things or external things?

Look at Philippians 4:11-13. Make these points:

- When he wrote these words Paul was in prison, probably facing a death sentence (see Philippians 1:12-14).

- Paul had once known privilege and prominence as a Roman citizen in the Jewish community. He said these things having 'been there and done that' (Philippians 3:4-6; Acts 22:3-5).

- Paul had suffered. He had been beaten, shipwrecked, stoned and jailed. He had also been disappointed spiritually (2 Corinthians 11:23-33).

Explain that Paul had experienced all extremes but was content. What was his secret?

Allow for suggestions and draw attention to his 'secret' in Philippians 4:13.

End by splitting the group into two teams and giving them one of the following passages each. Ask them to report back on its message:

- Luke 12:16-21 (satisfaction through material possessions is impossible to find).

- Luke 12:22-31 (true satisfaction comes through seeking God's kingdom first).

55. YOUTH

TRACK 4: Hey Young World (pt 2)

LENGTH: 4 mins 2 secs

IN BRIEF: A look at some of the challenges facing young people and how they can work to make tomorrow's world a better place.

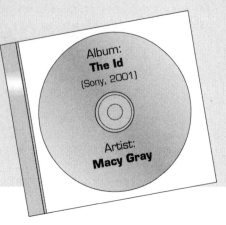

Album:
The Id
(Sony, 2001)

Artist:
Macy Gray

APPLICATION

You may wish to copy out the lyrics of the song onto OHP or flip chart paper before the session. Have them on view as the track is played.

PLAY THE TRACK > > > > >

Split the group into three smaller teams. Explain that each team is going to look at one particular verse of the song and explore a different issue raised in the song.

Give out one of the following to each team and allow 20 minutes for them to discuss the questions and read the verses. You will need to insert the full lyrics of the relevant song verse, as listed below:

INFLUENCE

Verse in song: second verse, starting 'Reward is a brainwashed kid . . . '

- Who influences you the most?
- Does having influence over someone equal having control over them?
- Is the old saying, 'bad company corrupts good character' true?
- Do you see school as 'yours'?
- List some of the good and bad influences which surround young people today.

Summarise the message of these passages in relation to influences:

Proverbs 4:23-27, Romans 8:5-8, Hebrews 11:24-28

ACCOMPLISHMENTS

Verse in song: third verse, starting 'Get ahead and accomplish things . . . '

■ Discuss a time when you have accomplished something. How did you feel?

■ Do you ever find yourself admiring people around you who are doing wrong but apparently accomplishing something?

■ What are your dreams for the next week, month and year?

■ Do you believe dreams come true?

Summarise the message of these passages in relation to accomplishment:

Ecclesiastes 3:1-8, Micah 6:8, James 1:26-27

GUIDANCE

Verse in song: last verse, starting 'Believe it or not . . . '

■ How does it make you feel knowing God 'watched you as you grew'?

■ What do the final three lines of the track mean?

■ How much of the direction your life takes do you put down to your decisions, or to God's guidance?

Summarise the message of these passages in relation to guidance:

Psalm 48:14, John 16:12-15, Proverbs 16:23

Come back together as a group and allow each team time to share what they discussed.

Play a game based around the chorus of the song: 'Hey young world, the world is yours.'

Divide into two teams. Team A is **'The World is Ours'** team, Team B is **'The World is Not Really Ours'** team. Appoint two people as judges.

Line both teams up at a starting point. Ask the following questions to both teams. Each must select a different person each time to present a response reflecting their team's view. The two judges decide which team presents the most convincing argument each time. That team then moves forward two steps. The winning team is the one to reach the finishing line first.

■ Power in the world does not only belong to the rich and politically powerful. There are ways that seemingly insignificant people groups can make themselves heard. Is this true?

■ The expectations of today's youth are so low that the idea of the world being theirs for the taking is ridiculous. Is this true?

■ It's not the person with the most convincing argument that is heard, but the person with the loudest voice. Is this true?

■ We underestimate the power of our own single voices. The Bible says that 'What you say can mean life or death' (Proverbs 18:21). Is this true for young people? Are young people really taken seriously enough to have a voice?

■ So many young people have set a bad example that the chance of 'youth' being taken seriously is a joke. Is this true?

■ The government do take young people seriously because they know they are the future voters. Is this true?

Sum up by saying: The world is there for the taking, but it requires energy, creativity and self-belief. The world is yours and you should live like it is yours for the taking.

56. FORGIVENESS

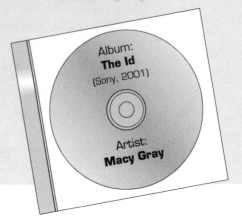

TRACK 12: Forgiveness

LENGTH: 5 mins 17 secs

IN BRIEF: A look at why it's important to forgive others.

Album:
The Id
(Sony, 2001)

Artist:
Macy Gray

APPLICATION

Introduce the theme by saying that you are going to be looking at one of the hardest things God expects of his followers. Don't say what it is, invite the group to listen out for it in the song.

PLAY THE TRACK > > > > >

Ask the group these questions after the track has finished and allow time for open discussion:

- Do we ever make promises we know we probably won't be able to keep, when we are really sorry for something and want forgiveness?
- In the track, Macy Gray says, 'please save some for me'. Does God's forgiveness ever run out?
- Are there ever occasions when our forgiveness should be withheld?

Ask a volunteer to read out the parable of the unmerciful servant in Matthew 18:21-35.

Invite the group to identify the different characters and how they might have felt.

Summarise by saying that we are like all the different characters in the story at different times. Sometimes:

- we are like the king and need to forgive others for significant wrongs they have done.
- we are like the man who owed the king 10,000 talents – millions of pounds. We need a lot of forgiveness ourselves.
- we are like the man who owed millions of pounds. We forget how much we have been forgiven, and refuse to forgive others the small thing they have done to us.
- we are like the man owing 100 denarii – a few pounds. We should still seek forgiveness for the thing we have done wrong.

Invite the group to think about which character best fits their situation at the moment.

PLAY THE TRACK AGAIN > > > > >

Replay the track as quiet background music. Invite the group to spend several minutes thinking about which character in the parable best mirrors their situation. Read out Matthew 6:9-15 emphasising that when we forgive, God forgives us. Encourage them to seek forgiveness from others if they need it.

PLAY THE TRACK AGAIN > > > > >

End by playing the track again. Invite the group to listen particularly to the section at 45 seconds where she talks about being washed down. Explain that this is the forgiveness God offers to us.

Does God's forgiveness ever run out?

57. MATCHMAKER GOD?

Album:
Music
(Maverick, 2000)

Artist:
Madonna

TRACK 4: I Deserve It

LENGTH: 4 mins 20 secs.

IN BRIEF: A chance to reflect on whether God is a matchmaker.

APPLICATION

ASK:

- Is God a matchmaker?
- What determines if something happening is from God, or by chance?

Read out the following scenarios and invite comment from the group:

- A friend of yours is planning a party at short notice. She needs a venue and believes God will provide one. You go into town on her behalf to look for one. After an hour of searching, you bump into a friend whose dad owns a club. She tells you that a booking they had for one of the rooms at the club has just cancelled – for the same night your friend needed a venue. Is this God's hand, or has he got bigger things to deal with? (Based on Mark 14:12-15.)

- Your family are Greek Orthodox. You have prayed that God will provide a marriage partner for you who will be a believer as well as sharing your Greek roots – as this is important to your parents. On your first night of freshers' week at university (where there is a large contingent of Greek students), you pray that God will cause you to cross paths with someone suitable. You are waiting at the bar when a girl starts up conversation with you. She turns out to be a Christian, and from a Greek orthodox family. Over time, things develop; you fall in love and marry. Was this a case of you looking so hard for something that you read the hand of God into circumstances? (Based on Genesis 24:12-14.)

Following on from the song, ask these questions:

- Do you use the phrase 'meant for'? What do you mean by it?
- Do you pray for a special someone you believe God has in store for you?
- Do you believe you were 'made for' just one particular person?

Split the group into teams. Give them the following verses and ask them to read and summarise the accounts:

TEAM A

- Mark 14:12-16 (The disciples 'find' the room for the Passover meal.)
- Genesis 24:1-18 (Abraham's servant 'meets' a wife for Isaac.)

TEAM B

- Jeremiah 2:1-19 (Israel forsakes God and pays a price.)

Explain that the fictional scenarios read out earlier were based on the passages looked at by Team A. The Bible does teach that God acts in and through the details of real life events. However, it also teaches that we can go our own way and step out of some of the good things lined up for us – as the Israelites did. Christians are called to do two things:

- Use our minds. God has given these tools to use, not to be set aside in the hope that God will bring everything about for us.

- Continue to obey and follow God. The often-quoted Jeremiah 29:11 has a clause in the following verse: 'Then you will call my name. You will come to me and pray to me.'

End with a time of prayer. Keep the group in small teams for this. Designate one end of the room 'my part' (in which they commit to following God and keeping their spiritual eyes and ears tuned to him), and the other 'God's part' (in which they pray for faith to know and see his hand in the nitty-gritty of life). Give them 5 minutes to spend praying in their teams.

58. SORRY, BUT

TRACK 6: Nobody's Perfect

LENGTH: 4 mins 58 secs

IN BRIEF: A chance to think about whether we mean 'sorry' when we say it.

Album:
Music
(Maverick, 2000)

Artist:
Madonna

PLAY THE TRACK > > > > >

Play the first 45 seconds of the track and pause it after the word 'sorry' but before the word 'but'.

Have a selection of teen/youth/fashion magazines spread on the floor. Invite the group to try to find 'sorry' in any of the magazines. Follow this up by inviting them to think of examples of public figures who have apologised for something of their own free will, i.e. without having been caught red-handed and therefore having been left with no choice but to apologise.

Explain that sorry is not an easy word to say. In society, it is often seen as a sign of failure and weakness rather than as a sign of wanting to do right and learn through mistakes.

PLAY THE TRACK AGAIN > > > > >

Play the track from the start again, and let it finish.

When it has finished, ask: 'What do the lyrics "nobody's perfect" and "I'm doing my best" really mean? Are these excuses for not wanting to own up to mistakes?'

Have a pile of heavy books in the room, along with a tough rucksack. Select a (fairly strong and outgoing) volunteer and have them put the rucksack on and stand with you in the centre.

Tell them that life is like a race (the volunteer takes up a starting position as if about to race). Whether it's at school, college, in your job, with your partner or on holiday, we all carry some worries, concerns and questions round with us. (Load some books in to represent these.) We add to these when we load ourselves down with things we know we've done wrong and owe apologies for, but don't want to say sorry (add several more books). When we need to say sorry but don't want to, we try to push it out of our minds or, like in the song, make excuses. But – the weight remains, slowing us down in our lives, and the longer it stays the heavier it gets (load some more books in).

Thank the volunteer and remove the bag. Give out a red (for 'I disagree') and green (for 'I agree') slip of paper to everyone. Explain that they must indicate their responses to the following statements using the slips:

- ■ In the Bible God once regretted a past decision. (TRUE: Genesis 6:5-6)

- ■ Saying sorry always seems hard but makes you feel ten times better when you've done it.

- ■ People feel that saying sorry is admitting their weakness.

- ■ Saying sorry is a start, not an end. It takes courage and shows strength.

Before ending with open prayer, emphasise that 'sorry, but . . . ' is not enough. God wants an honest sorry that goes deep. Use 2 Corinthians 7:10 as a stimulus to prayer.

God wants an honest sorry that goes deep

59. SUFFERING

TRACK 5: There By the Grace of God

LENGTH: 3 mins 47 secs

IN BRIEF: This session unpacks the can of worms that is suffering and looks at the role of God's grace in people's difficult times.

Album:
Forever Delayed
(Sony, 2002)

Artist:
Manic Street Preachers

APPLICATION

PLAY THE TRACK > > > > >

Invite the group to say what they think its message is. Refer to the chorus, which says: 'With grace we will suffer, with grace we will recover'.

Give out a selection of newspapers and magazines and ask them to look through and cut out any stories relating to suffering. As a group, they should work through the stories deciding which are suffering caused by the person's own actions, and which are suffering beyond that person's control. Place them in different piles.

Ask the group: 'Does God have less grace for people who bring suffering on themselves than for those who are victims of suffering beyond their control?'

Split the group into two and give one of the following to each group to consider:

SELF-INFLICTED SUFFERING

The Prodigal Son: Luke 15:11-32

- In what way was the son's suffering self-inflicted?
- Was the father's reaction to his son's return over-the-top?
- Was the brother justified in feeling annoyed?
- If you were the father, how would you have reacted when the son returned?
- What does this story teach about the characteristics of God's grace towards people who mess up?

SUFFERING OUTSIDE OF HUMAN CONTROL

The suffering of Job: Job 1:6-22 and 42:10-17

- Why do you think God allowed Job's suffering?
- If you were Job, how do you think you would have reacted towards God?
- How did God bless Job after his suffering?
- What does this story teach about God's grace?

Let the groups feed back. Explain that God gives his grace to all people in their difficult times, whether they are responsible for their suffering or not.

Brainstorm good things that can come out of suffering.

Look at the story of the blind man in John 9:1-12. Make these points to the group:

- Jesus made it clear that the man's suffering was not a punishment for sin. Rather it was an opportunity for God's glory to shine (John 9:3).
- Ask the group to brainstorm some of the good things that came about through the man's suffering and healing.

Explain that although some suffering brings good things, other suffering seems meaningless. Allow the group to share their own experiences of suffering. Encourage the group that it's OK to ask God why suffering happens. Introduce Habakkuk – a prophet who exchanged honest views with God about apparently unjust suffering.

Ask volunteers to read out:

- Habakkuk 1:2-4
- Habakkuk 1:12-17

Draw attention to the fact that:

- The Lord answered Habakkuk in chapter 2.
- Habakkuk was in a better place after bringing his questions to God – he confessed his faith in God again.

End by reading Habakkuk's confession of faith (Habakkuk 3).

PLAY THE TRACK AGAIN > > > > >

Remind them that it's in our suffering that God's grace can be most evident.

60. SUICIDE

TRACK 17: Suicide Is Painless

LENGTH: 3 mins 28 secs

IN BRIEF: This session looks at suicide, introducing some biblical principles on the sanctity of life.

Album:
Forever Delayed
(Sony, 2002)

Artist:
Manic Street Preachers

APPLICATION

Talk about reasons why young people commit suicide, obtaining a feel for your group's views on the subject. If it's an abstract issue for them, point out that it is a serious option for dealing with problems for increasing numbers of young people. Talk about the following statistics:

- Over the past 25 years, the suicide death rate among young men aged 15 to 25 has doubled. In 1974, 8 in 100,000 men aged 15-24 committed suicide. By 2000, that figure had risen to 16 in 100,000.

- Over the past 25 years, the suicide death rate among 15 to 25-year-old women has levelled out and remained stable. In 1974, 4 in 100,000 women aged 15-24 committed suicide. In 2000 that figure remained the same.

- According to the Samaritans, young men are 10 times more likely than young women to use drugs as an antidote to stress. US research has illustrated that one in three adolescents were intoxicated when they took their own life.

- Alcohol and drugs act as depressants. They lower inhibitions and, it is thought, increase the chances that a depressed young person who takes drugs will contemplate suicide.

Source: The Samaritans

If appropriate, you may wish to ask a question about whether any of the group has ever felt in such despair about something that suicide has flashed through their mind as an option.

Play the track and invite them to critically analyse the lyrics as they listen. Allow them to feed back their views of the track. Unpack the message of the song by asking the following:

- Is suicide really 'painless'?

- How desperate must people feel to take their own life?

- Do you agree with the Samaritans' research that young women are more likely to receive help and support from their peers if they share despondent and suicidal thoughts, than young men?

- What are some of the simple things in life that could help prevent suicidal thoughts?

Explain that the word suicide is not mentioned in the Bible and there is no specific teaching on it. However, several people are recorded in the Bible as having committed suicide:

King Saul and his armour bearer: 1 Samuel 31:4-5.

King Zimri of Israel: 1 Kings 16:18.

Judas took his own life after betraying Jesus: Matthew 27:5.

Explain that the Bible does lay out clear principles on the sacredness of life. Split the group into two and give one of the following to each to look at:

SACREDNESS OF LIFE

1. God's image: Genesis 1:27
2. God controls our birth and death: Job 1:21
3. We are God's temple: 1 Corinthians 6:19
4. God has decided our allotted life span: Psalm 139:16

HELP WHEN STRUGGLING

1. God comes close to those in need: Psalm 34:18
2. Jesus changes sadness to joy: Isaiah 61:1-3
3. There is hope: Proverbs 23:17-18
4. God's kingdom is about joy and peace: Romans 14:17

Allow feedback and then close by emphasising that suicide is not painless – it is a hard option taken by desperate people. It is also against God's teaching on the sacredness of life. Explain that suicidal thoughts are often made worse when people do not have friends to listen and care or when they do not take their difficulties to God.

Close with prayer. Be vigilant and sensitive towards any young people affected by the session.

127

. IDENTITY

TRACK 7: Little Girl

LENGTH: 2 mins 47 secs

IN BRIEF: To unpack the extent to which
we see ourselves as the sum of the
clothes we wear and image we project
and to examine how God sees us. Ideal as
a single-sex session. Lyrics for these
tracks are available at www.mary-mary.com.

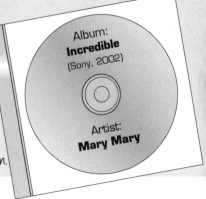

Album:
Incredible
(Sony, 2002)

Artist:
Mary Mary

APPLICATION

Start the meeting by asking everyone to spend several minutes looking at themselves closely – their hair, clothes, shoes, make-up (if they wear any), eyes, faces. Provide several mirrors for this purpose.

Ask: What makes you who you are? Do you see yourselves as the sum total of your clothes, make-up and hair? Do you see the 'hidden parts' – your inner identity – as a core part of who you are?

PLAY THE TRACK > > > > >

Give out mirrors to everyone. Instruct them to look at themselves and, as they do, to read the following:

> Look closely at yourself. God made you in his image.
> You are no mistake. God wanted you alive now, for a reason.
> He made you and knew you from when you were no bigger than an acorn.
> Look in the mirror. Look past the outer you and see your uniqueness.
> God's fingerprints are all over you. You were handmade by him.
> In the Bible, it says that our bodies were not hidden from God when we
> were being made.
> God assigned to us all our days.
> When he looks at you he sees beyond the clothes you wear. He sees the
> 'you' of you.
> He sees your heart, your emotions, and your unique personality.

(verses adapted from Psalm 139)

Have an open brainstorm around the word 'unique' and what it means. Give out printed/photocopied sheets of paper which have the following section of Psalm 139:13-14 (NCV) written on them: 'You formed me in my mother's body. I praise you because you made me in an amazing and wonderful way.'

PLAY THE TRACK AGAIN > > > > >

Have several inkpads, paper and tissues at the ready. Explain that unique means that there is no one the same as you. Place one of your fingers on the inkpad and make a fingerprint on the paper. As the track plays, meditate on this. Your identity is unique and something to be thankful to God for.

Have a bundle of old charity shop clothes (different to what the group would normally wear) at the ready. Ask for several volunteers. Instruct them to go into another room and put on the charity shop clothes.

When they return have them parade around the room.

Ask the rest of the group:

- ■ How does this change the way you see these people?

- ■ How much of the way you see people is determined by their outward appearance?

Ask the people dressed in the clothes:

- ■ How do you feel in these clothes?

- ■ Would it change the way you saw yourself as a person if you wore these clothes every day?

After they have changed out of the clothes, ask everyone to think about how long they spend in an average week on their outward appearance. Then ask them to think about how much time they devote each week to their inner identity – the inner them. Do they spend time reflecting on how they see themselves? Do they prepare the bit only God sees before they go out? Do they spend time thanking God for the uniqueness of the character he has given them? Encourage them not to neglect this.

Close the session with a time to share and pray. Make it a safe space for people to be open about their struggles in the area of identity. It may be that while some struggle with feelings of low self-confidence or self-image, others feel bad about the way they judge people on their clothing and outward appearance. Encourage the group to recognise that:

- ■ Clothing and outward appearance are not meaningless. They are important, but only part of the story.

- ■ Some people are unable to spend money on designer clothes.

- ■ We dishonour God – who made us as we are – when we don't value how God has made us or give time to developing this part of us.

62. LETTING GO

TRACK 15: Give It Up, Let It Go

LENGTH: 4 mins 2 secs

IN BRIEF: A chance for people to lift their worries, burdens and anxieties up to God.

Album:
Incredible
(Sony, 2002)

Artist:
Mary Mary

APPLICATION

This session ties into the verse 1 Peter 5:7 'Cast all your anxiety upon him for he cares for you'.

Have a pile of pebbles or stones in the centre of the room next to a sign saying 'Burdens I'm Carrying'. At another point in the room have a bucket with a label stuck on saying 'For God to Deal With'.

Also prepare some slips of paper (enough for 5 per person), some 4ft lengths of cotton (enough for one per person) and have sticky-tape at the ready.

PLAY THE TRACK > > > > >

Ask these questions:

- What's the message of the track?

- What sort of things make you feel worn out, burdened or are like weights on your mind?

- How do you let these things go when they are troubling you?

Tell the group that you are all going to take Jesus at his word. He told us to come to him when we were weary and burdened and he would give us rest. Think about things that are on your mind at the moment. Things that feel like a burden you are carrying. Take one stone from the pile to represent each of the things on your mind. On the slips of paper write each of these things and tape them to the piece of cotton.

PLAY THE TRACK AGAIN > > > > >

Play the track again while giving them 5 minutes to identify their burdens and write them on the paper.

When they have done this, produce a helium balloon. If resources stretch that far, have one per person. Assuming you have just one balloon, invite the group to tie their lengths of cotton with the paper strips stuck on it to the balloon.

When everyone has tied their own on, go into the garden or street. Have someone read 1 Peter 5:7 and then release the balloon. Encourage the group to see this as symbolic of them offering their worries and burdens up to God.

End with a time of prayer in which the group can symbolically place the stones they took representing their burdens into the bucket as a sign that they have given their problems up to God and that they are not going to walk away with them.

Jesus told us to come to him when we were weary and burdened and he would give us rest

63. HAS GOD LEFT ME?

Album:
18
(Mute, 2002)

Artist:
Moby

TRACK 2: In This World

LENGTH: 4 mins

IN BRIEF: A look at God's faithfulness — even when it feels like he's left us — through the lives of Jonah, Job and Elijah.

APPLICATION

PLAY THE TRACK > > > > >

Play the track and, as it ends, read Psalm 22:1-2

Divide the group into three clusters. Explain that you are looking at three characters that were all dependent on God's presence. Give one of the following to each group. Invite them to feed back their thoughts after 10 minutes:

JONAH: GOD'S UNWAVERING COMMITMENT

Jonah was a prophet sent by God to rebuke Nineveh. He had better ideas and fled in the opposite direction. Read Jonah chapter 1. Discuss these questions:

- Have you ever attempted to run from God? What happened?
- What does this account say about the possibility of 'fleeing from God'? How does this make you feel?
- What does the story say about the fear we might feel that God will leave us?
- Read verse 17. What was God's intention for Jonah – to punish or get him back on track?
- Read Jonah's description of God in verse 9. As a group, think up a contemporary description of God which takes into account his power over every element of life today from planes in the sky to virtual interaction between humans on the web.

JOB: TROUBLE DOESN'T EQUAL ABSENCE

Job was a godly man. God allowed him to be tested by the devil, but God never left him. Read Job chapter 23, where Job reflects on his situation and then read Job chapter 39:1-7 where God speaks to Job and reminds him that he sees and knows everything. Discuss these questions:

- How does Job deal with his feelings of not being able to find God in his situation (Job 23:11-12)?

- Why do you think God was not showing himself to Job during his trials?

- Do we try and box-in God too much? Job says, 'If only I knew where to find him' (ch.23:3). Is it more realistic to expect to meet God in different places and ways each day?

- How does God's giant perspective, as shown in Job 39:1-7, make you feel?

ELIJAH: GOD TURNS UP

God's prophets were being killed. Elijah was one of the few remaining. He called for a showdown between God and the false god Baal. Read 1 Kings 18:22-39 and discuss these questions:

- Elijah didn't seem put off by the fact that most of his fellow prophets had been killed by Ahab – the king he was now in the presence of. Was he naïve; did he have a death wish? What do you think made him take this risk?

- What would have happened if God hadn't shown up and sent the fire?

- Are there times when you have taken a risk and God has been faithful?

- How would you have reacted if you were Elijah and the fire had just fallen? Note Elijah's reaction in 1 Kings 19:3-4.

After each group has fed back, tell them that you are going to play the track again and read out verses about God's faithfulness over it. Invite them to use the time to respond to God and take on board what his word says.

Read a selection of these verses while the track plays: Psalm 22:1-2; Psalm 94:14; Deuteronomy 31:6; Hebrews 13:5-6.

End by asking them who the one person in the Bible was that God did forsake. Explain that it was Jesus, and read Matthew 27:46 where he feels the pain of separation from his father. Remind them that in being separated from God, Jesus dealt with the only thing that could separate us from him – sin.

64. COMMITMENT

TRACK 6: *One of These Mornings*

LENGTH: 3 mins 10 secs

IN BRIEF: This session looks at what real biblical friendship is and the role of commitment in being a good friend to other humans and to God.

Album:
18
(Mute, 2002)

Artist:
Moby

APPLICATION

The simple lyrics of this track can be used to good effect as an introduction to the subject of commitment and loyalty in friendships and relationships.

PLAY THE TRACK > > > > >

Give each person present a set of traffic light-coloured balloons: green (to represent yes/agree), yellow (to represent not sure/waiting) and red (to represent no/don't think so).

Read them the following statements. They must make their response by raising the balloon that corresponds to their answer. You may wish to ask for reasons why:

- More people than not of your age across the UK would say its fine to put down / end a friendship or relationship when it consistently stops serving their needs.

- In your social circle, it's considered OK to sleep with a partner as long as it's a long-term relationship.

- Looking at the state of typical marriages across the country, I never want to marry.

134

■ I believe that you get the most out of friendships when you are loyal and willing to commit for the long haul.

■ Friendship in the Bible is about sticking it out for the long haul.

■ Friendships do ebb and flow and there is a time when some friendships will go off the boil. In these situations, it's foolish to try to hang on to them.

Once the group has settled down, ask different members to read out these verses: Proverbs 17:17; Proverbs 27:10; James 2:23; John 15:13. Use these as the basis for a discussion and try to draw out some principles for friendship from the Bible. Cover the following areas:

■ What it means to be a friend of God.

■ What 'laying down your life' for a friend means in the here and now.

■ Knowing the difference between 'forsaking a friend' and simply accepting that things have gone off the boil.

■ Friendship is about giving, not just getting.

Close by dividing the group into pairs and encouraging them to discuss the ways in which they want to become a better friend to their peers and to God. Suggest they pray for each other and be accountable – reporting back in a week's time as to how they are getting on.

Friendship is about giving, not just getting

65. REGRETS

TRACK 15: A Little Deeper

LENGTH: 4 mins 35 secs

IN BRIEF: This session is designed to be done outside — though with little adaptation it can be used indoors. It tackles regrets and how to deal with them.

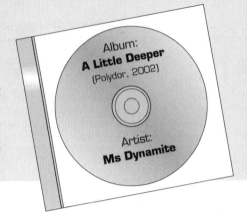

Album:
A Little Deeper
(Polydor, 2002)

Artist:
Ms Dynamite

APPLICATION

Start by asking if anyone has ever done something they later wished they hadn't? How did they deal with their regret?

Explain that you are going to play 'Stuck in the Mud'. Appoint one person the 'Sticker' and instruct the rest of the group to run from them. When someone is touched by the 'Sticker' they must stand with their arms outstretched in a cross shape until someone frees them by running under their right arm. Play a few rounds, appointing different people to be the 'Sticker'. The objective is to get everyone stuck in the mud and unable to run about.

After the game, explain that regrets can be like the 'Sticker' in the game – they cause us to get stuck where we are and to stop moving on in our lives. However, the Bible teaches that we should not allow regrets to control our actions – Jesus should be the one who directs our lives.

Look at these two passages with the group:

    1. Ecclesiastes 11:1-4.

    2. Isaiah 40:29-31

PLAY THE TRACK > > > > >

Use the following lines from it as discussion starters:

- 'I was hiding from me'. Is this a clue as to why we can't let some regrets go – because we find it hard to face up to what we have done?

- 'Dig a little deeper within u'. How important is our will in moving beyond regret? Can looking within help you move on outwardly?

- 'Think a little deeper bout what u do'. Are things we do which we later regret usually things done quickly and in haste, or after a lot of thought? What can we learn from this?

Ask the group:

- Does God ever have regrets? Allow them to brainstorm ideas then give out Genesis 6:5-8 as an example of God being sorry for something he did.

- Did Jesus have regrets? Read out the description of Jesus in Isaiah 53:3 as a 'man of sorrows' who was 'despised'. Ask them whether they think he ever regretted taking up the mission to come to earth and save us.

Have a barbecue or bonfire ready (if you are indoors, use an empty dustbin). You will also need some superglue handy. Have two pieces of wood with **'You'** written on one and **'Your Regrets'** written on the second in marker pen.

Tell the group that when we make mistakes we have two choices. We can either internalise the mistake, dwell on it and let it affect us, or we can face up to it, learn from it and move on. When you fail to let a mistake go you are refusing the forgiveness that God offers you. Instead, you are holding the regret close to you until it sticks and becomes part of who you are.

At that point, the leader should smear superglue on the **'Your Regrets'** piece of wood and stick it to the **'You'** piece of wood.

Conclude the illustration by reading 2 Corinthians 7:10 from the NIV and then splitting the wood apart using a hammer and screwdriver. Make the point that the more we let regrets become part of us, the harder it will be to remove them. Throw the **'Your Regrets'** piece of wood in the fire/barbecue and re-read 2 Corinthians 7:10 as it burns.

Conclude the session by giving out pens and paper. Give them 10 minutes to think through any regrets they might be holding onto and to write them down. Invite them to throw the paper into the fire/barbecue as a symbol of offering them to God and accepting his forgiveness. As they do this, read Jeremiah 29:11.

66. CHANGE

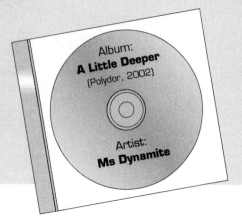

TRACK 13: *Gotta Let U Know*

LENGTH: 4 mins 8 secs

IN BRIEF: This session looks at what causes people to want to change.

Album:
A Little Deeper
(Polydor, 2002)

Artist:
Ms Dynamite

APPLICATION

PLAY THE TRACK > > > > >

Start by playing the track. Invite the group, as they listen, to pick out any lines that relate to change. Look through the lyrics on the CD inlay – there are plenty there.

Ask the group whether any of them have ever wanted to change someone they know, and if so, how they went about it. Did it work?

Draw attention to the last line in the chorus which talks about only being able to help someone change if they want to change themselves.

Ask everyone to take their shoes off and place them in front of them. Pick on several different people and tell them they must make their shoes do what they were made to do – walk – without touching them. Give them a few minutes to try and then ask them to shout at their shoes and command them to move. When nothing happens, explain that we are a bit like our shoes. It is what's on the inside of us that determines whether we do what we were made to do. If your foot is not in your shoe, the shoe will not go anywhere. If it is, and you decide you want to go somewhere then the shoe will be empowered to move. It's the same with people. For people to change they need to have something inside of them that wants to change. Without that motivation, they will be like an empty shoe.

We change when we are motivated to do so

138

Look at the story of Zacchaeus as a case study for change. Read Luke 19:1-10 and discuss these questions as a group:

- What was Jesus' strategy for bringing change into Zacchaeus' life?
- What do you think was at the heart of Zacchaeus' transformation?
- What does the story teach us about helping people change their ways?

Sum up by saying that we change when we are motivated to do so. We get motivated when we see someone else changing in the way we want to. Suddenly change is being lived out in front of us and it becomes possible and attractive. If you want to change someone, live out that change in yourself first.

Give out paper and pens and ask the group to write down the following two rules of change to take away and think through when they want to see change:

- Is there motivation for change? Is that motivation stronger in the person you want to change, or in you?
- Have you made sure you have begun to change and develop in your own life in the area you want the other person to change in?

If you want to change someone, live out that change in yourself first

67. HALF-HEARTED DISCIPLESHIP

TRACK 12: *Overboard*

LENGTH: 5 mins 16 secs

IN BRIEF: This session is about how we respond to the message of God's kingdom.

Album:
Colour Scheme
(Alliance, 2002)

Artist:
Nicki Rogers

APPLICATION

A week before doing this session, grow four sets of cress seeds following these instructions:

- ■ Put a set on a saucer with a small amount of water but no cotton wool, so that they start to germinate but do not grow properly (like character 1, below).
- ■ Grow a second set on damp cotton wool but when they have started growing starve them of water so that by the time of the meeting they look withered (like character 2, below).
- ■ Grow a third set in damp cotton wool, but when they are becoming established, restrict their stems using paper clips (like character 3, below).
- ■ Allow a final set to grow normally on damp cotton wool (like character 4, below).

Introduce the track by explaining that it is about one person's journey from a place where they didn't really notice God around them, to a place where they have accepted his message and gone overboard – all-out – for Christ.

PLAY THE TRACK > > > > >

Ask for a volunteer to read the parable of the sower from Mark 4:1-9. Ask the group for ideas on what Jesus was trying to say through it.

Have another volunteer read out Jesus' explanation of the parable from Mark 4:14-20 and then say that in the parable the seeds represent all of the people who hear the message. Jesus implies that even those who have it snatched away by Satan have understood something about the kingdom of God. We are going to look at what Jesus is saying to us about not settling for half-hearted discipleship.

Divide into four groups. Unpack the four types of people described in the parable and, as you do, produce the appropriate cress seeds to illustrate the effect this approach has.

1. Hardened like the path. The seed cannot take root and is snatched by Satan.

2. Joyful but short-lived in the face of difficulties.

3. Pulled away by worries, wealth and other concerns.

4. Accepted the word and produced a good crop.

Allocate these four types of people in the parable, one to each team. Give each group a marker pen and a 7ft length of plain wallpaper. Explain that they must draw around one of their team on the wallpaper and then write onto the outline the characteristics of the type of person they have been allocated. Give them Bibles so they can re-read what Jesus said about their character. Encourage them to think about what a person who responds to the word in that way might be like. For example, the group doing character number 1 might write words like: closed, a bit of a know-it-all, proud.

When they have written their words on their outline, allow time for them to feed back and explain.

Invite the group to reflect honestly on their own attitude to the message of Jesus. If they feel confident enough, they should then write their name on a post-it note and stick it onto the character type they think most reflects where they are at.

Explain that wherever we are at, Jesus' message is one of change. He came for sinners, not for perfect people. Tell them that you are going to play the track again, giving them an opportunity, if they want to, to open their heart like fertile soil for Jesus to grow and live in; to invite him to break up the hard bits in their life.

Jesus' message is one of change

After the track has finished, explain that those who did invite Jesus to break the hard parts of their heart should expect that he will do that – and that he will do that through challenging experiences they face this week.

68. GRAINS OF SAND

TRACK 10: *Ocean*

LENGTH: 5 mins 27 secs

IN BRIEF: This session is designed to be done at the beach. However, it could be adapted for use indoors.

Album:
Colour Scheme
(Alliance, 2002)

Artist:
Nicki Rogers

APPLICATION

This session could be used well to conclude a group day at the beach. Use a battery-powered CD player.

If you cannot get to the beach, you might want to think about getting some sacks of sand (from a DIY centre) and laying them out on polythene. For the waves, consider videoing them when on holiday in preparation for the session.

Look at the sand across the beach and thank God for his knowledge of, and interest in you

PLAY THE TRACK > > > > >

Invite the group to listen and reflect on the words. When it has finished, ask them to brainstorm what they think the singer meant by the line 'In your ocean I am found' and 'pull me safely to the warmth of your strong shores'. Allow for discussion.

Invite the group to listen to the sound of the waves, to look at the expanse of the ocean and to think about what they say about God. After 5 minutes, invite people to share thoughts.

Explain that in the Bible the ocean is often used to help explain truths. Divide them into four groups, giving each small group one of the following passages to read and discuss. Encourage them to spend time looking at the sea and its waves when reading the passage to visually grasp the truth being explained:

- Psalm 93:3-4: (God is greater than the might of the sea and its waves).

- Micah 7:18-19: (God buries our sin in the depths of the ocean).

- James 1:5-6: (A person who doubts God is like a wave on the sea – unstable in all they do).

- Job 11:7-9: (God's mysteries are wider than the ocean).

Come back together as one group and invite each of the smaller groups to share what the passage they studied said about the ocean.

Invite everyone to take a handful of sand and try to count the grains of sand in their palm by transferring them one by one back to the beach. If the beach you are on is pebbly, suggest they try to count all pebbles on the beach.

After 5 minutes, call a halt. Ask them to look at the sand (if the beach you are on is pebbly, substitute 'sand' for 'pebbles') as you read the following meditation:

> *God knows exactly how many grains of sand there are on this beach, and on every beach in the world.*
>
> *Think for a minute: if God knows this information, how much more does he know every detail of your life – the good and the bad. He loves you and knows you intimately.*
>
> *Look at the sand across the beach and thank God for his knowledge of, and interest in you.*

Conclude by reading Genesis 22:17.

69. SIGNS OF GOD

TRACK 8: Lonestar

LENGTH: 3 mins 5 secs

IN BRIEF: This session is designed to be done outside, under the stars. It looks at signs of God's presence and power.

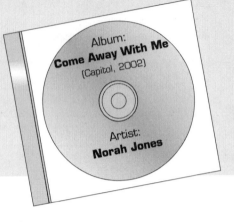

Album:
Come Away With Me
(Capitol, 2002)

Artist:
Norah Jones

APPLICATION

This velvety jazz number raises the issue of feeling alone and wishing for some kind of sign that you are not alone. This session would have the best impact done outside under a starry sky. If possible, use someone's garden or go to a common. Use a battery powered portable CD player for the sound.

Start with a game of hide and seek in twos. Send pairs off (with torches if you are on public land) to hide. After several minutes, send the finding pair after them. The finding pair are allowed to use a torch to identify where the pairs are hiding.

After the game, gather everyone together and sit/stand in silence for several minutes gazing at the stars in the sky.

PLAY THE TRACK > > > > >

Explain that sometimes it feels like we would give anything for God to give us some sort of sign to show us we're not alone. Like the game of hide and seek, it can feel like we have been left in the dark and are waiting for him to shine down on us.

Do you ever forget the majesty and size of God?

Follow this up with a discussion looking at how God can be so close when the expanse above us is so huge. Use these questions to spark the discussion:

- Where is God now?
- Look up into the heavens God created. Do you ever forget the majesty and size of God?
- Have you ever felt like you would give anything just for God to shine down on you?
- What distance would you go to meet God? Are there examples of ways you have pushed the boat out to try and draw near to God?

PLAY THE TRACK AGAIN > > > > >

As the track finishes, read Psalm 139:7-12 several times, allowing it to sink in. Pick up on verse 12 and say that to God the darkness which restricts our view is light. He can see in the dark! He sees all we do and is so close to us that we often look in the wrong places for evidence of his presence.

Ask the group how and where they look for signs of God's presence.

Follow this up by asking them where God lives? Have Ephesians 3:16-17 printed on card and ask a volunteer to read it using a torch.

Make the point that although the universe is so huge, God actually lives in our hearts. Sometimes we look around for signs of him, but forget to look inside at our own lives for evidence of his activity.

Read out the second (last) verse of the track from the CD inlay and explain that you are going to look at what the Bible says about signs and how we should seek them.

Have someone read Matthew 12:38-40 and explain that Jesus is the sign we should hold on to. His death and resurrection is a promise between God and his people (us) that he will never leave us alone – that he will live in our hearts and through our lives.

PLAY THE TRACK AGAIN > > > > >

End by playing the track a final time and re-reading Psalm 139:7-12.

70. MANIC LIFE

TRACK 13: The Long Day is Over

LENGTH: 2 mins 44 secs

IN BRIEF: This session is about when life seems hyper and manic — and meeting God in the middle of it. You should tell everyone that they need to bring a cushion or pillow with them to the meeting.

Album:
Come Away With Me
(Capitol, 2002)

Artist:
Norah Jones

APPLICATION

Start by having a 'manic minute'. Explain that each person must think up a manic activity for the person on their left, which can be done within the confines of the meeting area. It could be anything from press-ups or running on the spot to singing their favourite song loudly.

At the word 'go', each person must throw themselves into the manic activity for one minute.

Follow this up by telling everyone they can sit and relax now. Ask them how the activity made them feel. Has this week been manic and made them feel this way? Allow time for them to talk about any ways in which their week and their lives seem manic at the moment.

Explain that you are going to play a very relaxing track called 'The Long Day is Over' to help them unwind. Ask them all to lie down comfortably with their heads on their pillows and to imagine something peaceful like the sun rising.

Imagine something peaceful like the sun rising

PLAY THE TRACK > > > > >

Play the track several times.

Give out paper and pens or, if you are feeling ambitious, lay out sheets and set up a paint area with a roll of blank wallpaper and paints. Invite the group to depict themselves, through art, in a way that reflects how they feel life is at the moment. They must not draw themselves, but draw an object or shape to reflect how they feel: if life is hectic, they might draw a cluttered bedroom; if they feel at bursting point, they might draw an over inflated balloon; if life is calm, they might draw a bird soaring through the air. Encourage them to think outside the box.

After 10 minutes, go round the room and allow each person to share their picture and what it is saying about how they feel.

Give the group time to relax. Then read Psalm 23. Invite them to draw or paint another image – this time to represent the element of Jesus, as depicted in the Psalm, that most appeals to them. Again, encourage them not to draw him as a person, but to draw an object or scene to represent how they see Christ.

Ask the group to share creative ways they have found to meet God when they are feeling manic and over-run. Have a few up your own sleeve including:

- Set a time each day to have just one minute of being silent and thinking of the image of Christ they painted.

- Find someone in the group to meet to pray with on a regular basis.

- Remember Psalm 23:2-3. God is the one who can bring real restoration to your soul and peace into your life.

End with a time when the group can pray for each other. Use the pictures or paintings that each person drew to reflect how they were feeling as a stimulus for what they should pray for each other.

God is the one who can bring real restoration to your soul and peace into your life

71. A HEALTHY SOUL

TRACK 6 (CD2): Mekka

LENGTH: 6 mins 3 secs

IN BRIEF: A chance for the group to look inside themselves and feed and water their souls.

Album:
Travelling
(Perfecto, 2000)

Artist:
Paul Oakenfold

APPLICATION

This popular dance track provides great background sound for an exploration of the soul. The aim of this session is for people to consider what state their soul is in, to identify some of the things that dry it out and to re-connect with God, allowing him to feed their soul.

You will need: enough copies of the meditation below for one per person; enough good apples for one per person; a bowl of rotten apples (you may need to store these several weeks to get them rotten enough); plastic knives and plates for people to use to cut up the apples; paper and pens.

PLAY THE TRACK > > > > >

While it is playing give out the following meditation to each young person. Tell them to read it and interact with it at their own pace. You may need to repeat the track several times depending on how long the group need.

> *In front of you is an apple.*
> *Cut it in half.*
> *Look at the core*
> *The core is the central part of this apple.*
> *It is the essence, the heart of the apple.*
> *It is where new life comes from – note the apple seeds waiting to produce new life.*
> *Your soul is like the core of this apple.*

Your soul is the central part of you.
It is your essence, the heart of you.
It is where God pours in new life.

Take a moment to reflect on your core, your soul.
How does it feel at the moment?
Is there joy or sadness, life or death, peace or trouble?
Are you feeling hyper on the outside, but a bit dried up on the inside?

When an apple detaches from its source – the tree – it begins to rot.
The tree supplies it with food and water.
When this is interrupted, the life is squeezed out of its core.
Its skin turns brown and it is no longer useful.
Look at the rotten apples.

We are similar to apples in this way: when we become detached from
our source – God – our souls begin to rot.
If we neglect the food and water that our source can bring, then we
experience the life being squeezed out of our souls.
We become drained and empty, and our souls are deprived of Jesus.

Identify some of the things that turn your core rotten:
Is it your love of money or things you own?
Is it the films or programmes you watch on TV?
Is it your lack of connection with God?
Is it your lack of self-control that leads you away from God?

Write some of the things you think rot your core down on the paper.

Take some time now to focus on the core of your being and on its life-
giving source.
Your core is your soul.
Your source is God.
Now identify how you can help your soul to stay close to its source.

In John 15, Jesus described himself as a vine and us as the branches – attached to him and drawing nourishment from him. Spend a few minutes praying and re-connecting with the source of life.

As you go away, hold the image in your head of the good apples and their core. Remember that when you stay close to your source – God – your soul has life.

End the session by reading out John 15:5-6 and having a prayer time where people can re-connect with God.

72. ICEBREAKERS

TRACK 1 (CD 1): Velvet Girl

LENGTH: 7 mins 50 secs

IN BRIEF: These session ideas will serve as great icebreakers for a new group at the start of a term. They will help everyone find out about each other and get acquainted. This Paul Oakenfold track (and others on the album) will help create a buzz in the atmosphere.

Album:
Travelling
(Perfecto, 2000)

Artist:
Paul Oakenfold

APPLICATION

PLAY THE TRACKS > > > > >

Play the CEILING-BALLOON GAME by tying 10 balloons to the ceiling (the higher the ceiling the better). In each balloon put flour or shredded paper. Divide the group into two teams. Taking it in turns, each team fields a player to try to burst one of the balloons. Give the contestant a long pole with a pin sellotaped to the end to burst the balloon with. The contestant must be blindfolded and disorientated (spin them round several times). They then have 30 seconds to burst a balloon. Their team can shout directions to them.

Play the GONG GAME by splitting them into groups of about three and tell them to come up with a name for their team. They then have 5 minutes to decide on 10 subjects, 1 of which they will ask the person in the 'hot seat' to talk on for 1 minute (vary this time to suit your group).

Set up a hot seat and a candidate from one of the teams. One of the other teams then gives them a subject to talk on. If they hesitate for more than 3 seconds, bang the gong. Each team has 10 points to start with. They lose 1 every time a member fails to complete the minute. The winner is the team with the most left at the end.

The FOOT-BALLOON GAME involves tying an inflated balloon round everyone's ankle. Split the group into two teams and on the word go, the two teams must battle it out to burst as many of the other side's balloons as possible. Once someone's balloon is burst, they must sit out.

Try the EGG GAME. Send three people out of the room and bring one in. show them a line of eggs they must walk through without breaking any. Blindfold them and encourage those watching to shout directions and make sounds to indicate when they are nearly treading on the eggs. The catch is this – remove the eggs as soon as they are blindfolded and replace them just before they take the blindfold off. The group will enjoy watching them think they are about to break an egg and avoiding objects that are not there. Let them in on the secret after and thank them for being good sports. ---> ---> ---> --->

These session ideas will serve as great icebreakers for a new group at the start of a term

73. MY OWN WAY

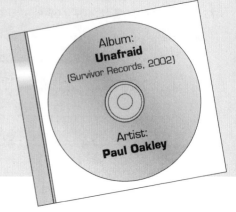

TRACK 13: Adam's Race

LENGTH: 13 mins 31 secs

IN BRIEF: A chance to look at what Adam and Eve's sin means for us and at God's offer of a second chance.

Album:
Unafraid
(Survivor Records, 2002)

Artist:
Paul Oakley

APPLICATION

Start with an exercise to illustrate how we reflect our ancestors in the way we look. Go round the room picking on different people and asking where they trace their jaw line, nose shape, hair or eye colour, shape of mouth, height and build from. Do the same exercise for personality preferences, sense of humour and particular abilities.

The objective is to help the group see that elements of who we are, are passed down to us. We reflect in how we look and through some of our actions and interests, elements of our forefathers and mothers, although we don't know this because they are not around to tell us.

PLAY THE TRACK > > > > >

Explain that the same principle of inheriting characteristics from our ancestors applies to the selfish characteristics which are part of us, passed down since Adam and Eve disobeyed God. We are going to unpack our family tree and look at how Adam and Eve's disobedience affects us.

Split the group into three teams, giving one of the following to each:

TEAM 1: THE SIN OF ADAM AND EVE

Romans 5:12-14   Genesis 3:1-8   Hosea 6:7

- When did sin reign and how did it come to reign?

- What did it mean that Adam and Eve's eyes 'were opened'?

- What had Adam and Eve broken by eating the fruit?

TEAM 2: THE EFFECTS OF ADAM AND EVE'S SIN

Genesis 6:5-8 Romans 5:12-14

- In what way were Adam and Eve a 'pattern' for all future humans?
- How did God feel about the disobedience of humanity?

TEAM 3: THE NEW PLAN FOR HUMANS

1 Corinthians 15:20-22 Romans 5:15-19

- How did God sort the mess out?
- What was the result of Jesus' 'one act of righteousness'?

Allow each group to share their findings.

Ask the group: 'What things in life tempt you and draw you to them? What are the things that you would like to spend more time on?'

Make the point that Adam and Eve were drawn to the fruit. The fact that it was there, in front of them, to touch, made it more attractive than God's command not to eat the fruit, which probably seemed distant and less important.

Challenge them to bring God's word to life, to make it a real, lively, important part of their life, which they see daily as well as remember in their hearts. Give out the following verses for them to look up: Deuteronomy 6:5; Matthew 22:37-39; Micah 6:8.

They should select a verse that strikes them and then spend 5 minutes thinking through how to translate the message of the verse into a clay sculpture. Provide clay for this purpose and allow 20 minutes for sculpting. Let the models dry and give them out at a future session. Encourage them to keep the sculptures to remind them of the importance of obeying God.

Close by asking the question which the song raises: 'In Adam's or Eve's shoes what would you have done?'

What things in life tempt you and draw you to them?

74. BELIEF

TRACK 10: Jerichos

LENGTH: 3 mins 32 secs

IN BRIEF: A look at the story of Jericho and at the principle in our discipleship of believing God can do big things.

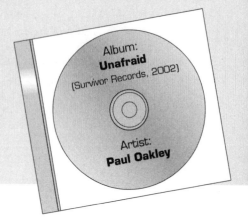

Album:
Unafraid
(Survivor Records, 2002)

Artist:
Paul Oakley

APPLICATION

Most of this session will be done in teams. Split the group into four teams: Matthew, Mark, Luke and John. If the group is not big enough for four groups, just have two or three teams and adapt the exercises.

Start with an icebreaker. Give each team three newspapers and a roll of sellotape. Tell them they have 5 minutes to build the tallest, freestanding tower. When the time is up the teams must stand away from their towers. Award a prize to the one whose tower is tallest.

Read Joshua 6:15-20.

PLAY THE TRACK > > > > >

Invite people to comment on the message they think is coming through the song.

Explain that the triumphant story of Jericho started with Joshua's willingness to take God at his word, even though the material facts of a fortified city didn't seem to add up.

Read Joshua 6:1-8 and point out that if Joshua had not believed God and acted, Jericho would never have fallen. Make the point that God often expects us to start responding to his word before he will unravel the next part of the plan.

Ask a volunteer to read John 14:12 in which Jesus tells his followers that they will do greater things than he did.

With the group still in their four teams, tell them they have 5 minutes to look through the book of the Bible which their team is named after. They must make a list of the all the things that Jesus did, from healings to preaching to praying, which are listed in that book.

After they have done this, allow each team to feed back. Write their findings on a flipchart/OHP. Ask the group to come up with a number between 1 (unlikely) and 4 (very likely) to represent how likely they think it is that they would do a similar thing in society today. Write the number on the flipchart/OHP next to the act it refers to.

You will probably find, if members of the group are being honest, that there are plenty of 1s and 2s written up. Provide a short summary of how we are called as disciples to approach 'Jerichos' we face in our own lives:

- Jesus did not intend for his words in John 14:12 to place heavy expectations on his followers. Rather, he wanted them to look at life at a deeper level and tune into his activity.

- As with Joshua and Jericho, he simply had to listen, tune in, and obey what he thought God wanted him to do. It is helpful to see our journey towards doing the things Jesus did as just that – a journey.

- Jesus called his followers to view the whole of their lives as a mission to know him and make him known. The supernatural intervention of God as they did this was, and is, part of this package.

Close by reminding them that it's when we obey God in the small things that he reveals his bigger plan to us.

It's when we obey God in the small things that he reveals his bigger plan to us

75. MISUNDERSTOOD

TRACK 3: Missundaztood

LENGTH: 3 mins 36 secs

IN BRIEF: This session deals with how people are misunderstood, why misunderstandings happen and ways to respond to being misunderstood.

Album:
Missundaztood
(Arista, 2002)

Artist:
Pink

APPLICATION

Divide the group into two. Give a copy of a tabloid newspaper and of the Daily Telegraph from the same day to both groups. Give one group John 2:13-16 and the other Luke 14:25-27. Instruct them to spend several minutes looking in the papers at how stories are reported and then imagine they are non-Christian journalists sent to report on Jesus from the account in the passage. They know nothing about Jesus beyond what they are seeing of him now. Their Editor wants a juicy story.

Give each small group 10 minutes to write a newspaper story based around the Bible passage.

Follow this up by giving each group 5 minutes to come up with as many examples of how stories are reported differently in the tabloid and the broadsheet you gave them.

Ask them why they think the stories are different. Help them to see that how you perceive an event will depend on where you are standing – your beliefs and attitudes and how well you know and understand the people involved. Would Jesus have felt misunderstood in the story they wrote?

PLAY THE TRACK > > > > >

Play the track then invite any in the group who want to, to share times they have felt misunderstood and how they responded.

Explain that you are going to look at misunderstanding. Brainstorm the following:

- Reasons why people are misunderstood.
- Examples of public figures who have been misunderstood.
- Examples of when Jesus was misunderstood and how he reacted.

Have a volunteer read out Mark 15:1-5 where Jesus is silent before Pilate, and Mark 8:14-21 where Jesus tries to make himself understood to the disciples. Make the point that sometimes Jesus did try to explain and clarify what he meant but he rarely tried to vindicate himself in the face of false accusations or people misunderstanding him.

Split the group into two teams. Give them 10 minutes to prepare their arguments for a debate. One side must argue for why it is better to stay silent when misunderstood and the other side for why it is important to speak out to clarify misunderstandings. Give each side 5 minutes to present their side and allow for questions from those listening.

Arrange the group in a line down the room and play Chinese Whispers using these phrases:

- 'I have 96 sausages in my fridge at home and I'm going to eat them all tonight.'
- 'My ambition for next month is to visit space and experience weightlessness.'
- 'When I have chips I cover them in salt, ketchup and vinegar. Vinegar is good as a disinfectant.'

When finished, conclude by emphasising these points:

- We misunderstand people because we don't listen carefully to what they are really saying.
- We misunderstand people when we repeat or listen to things said about them without asking them whether it is true and what they meant.

76. HAPPY FAMILIES?

TRACK 8: *Family Portrait*

LENGTH: 4 mins 56 secs

IN BRIEF: This session deals with the sometimes-hard reality of modern-day family life and looks at God's principles for the family.

Album:
Missundaztood
(Arista, 2002)

Artist:
Pink

APPLICATION

Give out paper and pencils. Instruct everyone to draw a portrait of their family, but with their eyes shut. Invite everyone to show their artwork.

Explain that this session looks at the family and some of the challenges we face being part of families. Be inclusive – explain that some people's family has two parents and some have one.

PLAY THE TRACK > > > > >

Before the meeting prepare several people-paper-chains based on the following descriptions:

- ■ One chain of 5 people, all linked (representing a family in which the members get along quite well).

- ■ One chain of 5 people with some of the arms or legs between the people cut so they are only loosely attached (representing a family in which there are tensions and divisions).

- ■ One chain of 5 people with some broken links (representing members of a family separated from other members, perhaps through divorce).

Invite the group to spend a few minutes thinking in their own minds which paper chain best fits their family situation. If appropriate, ask people to share how they see their family situation.

Have a game of piggy in the middle in which a tennis ball is thrown between two groups of people and the person in the centre must try and catch it. Then, using the song lyrics in the CD inlay, read from the start down to the line 'this is my shelter'.

Explain that sometimes it can feel like we are caught in the crossfire in our families or that we are playing piggy in the middle. Though we wish our families were places of shelter, we feel like we need to take shelter from them.

Read out Psalm 68:5-6 and tell the group that God's intention was that families were places where we find security and comfort. Although the reality is often different, God's intentions have not changed. We are going to look at some principles God has laid out for families to help us in our families now and for the future when we start our own families.

Split the group into two smaller clusters. Give them the following verses and instruct them to note down what each verse says about the family. Be very aware that young people from dysfunctional families may have trouble relating to this:

GROUP 1

Matthew 15:4: God wants people to honour their parents.

Luke 14:26: God's call on our lives must take precedence over our family.

Hebrews 12:7-8: The family is the place for discipline and learning.

Proverbs 4:3-6: The family is where wisdom is taught.

GROUP 2

1 Timothy 5:4: It pleases God when grown-up children care for their aged parents.

Proverbs 23:22: We should listen to and not despise our parents.

Ephesians 6:1-4: Guidance for parents and children.

Deuteronomy 6:6-9: Family is the place where God's commands are taught.

Draw a line down the centre of a large sheet of flip chart paper. Ask the groups to feed back their findings and write them on one side of the flip chart paper. Invite the group to throw in suggestions which compare what the Bible says on the one side, to the accepted view of the family in popular culture today, which you should write on the other side of the line.

End by making these points:

- Conflict happens in every family – it is inevitable.

- Families make mistakes, but God doesn't give up on them. The very first family in the Bible was Adam, Eve, and their two sons, Cain and Abel. Cain murdered his brother Abel (Genesis 4:8) out of jealousy, but God still looked after Cain (Genesis 4:13-16).

- The family was God's invention and he can work in any family, however problematic.

77. CONFESSION

TRACK 5: Merciful

LENGTH: 5 mins

IN BRIEF: To unpack what confession is, what we need to confess, and why it's important.

Album:
Transform
(Forefront, 2000)

Artist:
Rebecca St James

APPLICATION

Start by asking the group to brainstorm typical confessions people make, and the people they make these confessions to. Write the suggestions on a flip chart/OHP and then take a vote on reasons why people confess. Is it:

    (a) because they know they have been found out?

    (b) because of guilt and a genuine desire to put things right?

PLAY THE TRACK > > > > >

Explain that the track is about confessing sin to God and seeking his mercy. What are the things Rebecca St James refers to which require confession?

Allow time for them to make suggestions and if necessary play the track again.

Refer back to the list the group drew up of things people make confession for, and then contrast that with the focus of this track – confessing things left undone (58 seconds into the track).

Either play the track again or read the lyrics from the CD inlay and as a group identify:

- What 'sins' are flagged up? (*Not loving God with the whole of our hearts; things left undone.*)

- What response is suggested in the song? (*Laying down (as a sign of repentance); crying out to God (praying); asking for mercy and forgiveness; doing what we should have done, but didn't; walking in God's ways; lifting God's name high.*)

Ask: Why do we tend to think of confession in terms of wrong things we have done, rather than good things we have left undone?

Have volunteers read out Malachi 3:6-10, John 12:42-43 and 2 Corinthians 9:12-13 and make these points:

- In Malachi, the people were robbing God – sinning – by not bringing enough food to the sanctuary.
- God assured them that if they made amends he would bless them abundantly. This is a biblical principle.
- In John 12, the leaders failed to confess Christ because of their fear of becoming unpopular.
- In 2 Corinthians, the people did what they should have done and this spread the gospel.

In preparation for the meeting, you and some friends should record, on tape, a 'late night radio confessions show' with a difference. Make it a phone-in with the presenter who has invited listeners to call in with their confessions. Have the presenter introduce the show and invite listeners to phone in confessions of things they have done wrong. Arrange for four or five different people to call in, all saying they haven't done anything but still feel the need to confess. Their confessions could be linked to something like not buying a copy of the *Big Issue* from someone who looked cold and hungry or not offering to do shopping for the old lady next door when she broke her hip. Use your imagination!

Play the recording to the group and then brainstorm any things people in the group feel they should have done, but have not.

Read 1 John 1:9 and end with a time of prayer. Encourage the group to go away and think through things they can do for God that they have not been doing.

Why do we tend to think of confession in terms of wrong things we have done, rather than good things we have left undone?

78. BEING DISTINCTIVE

TRACK 3: Reborn

LENGTH: 3 mins 57 secs

IN BRIEF: To unpack what we mean by being distinctive as Christians and brainstorm how we can be distinctive without being weird.

Album:
Transform
(Forefront, 2000)

Artist:
Rebecca St James

APPLICATION

Start by brainstorming answers to the question 'what makes a Christian different and distinctive?' Follow this by asking who thinks that some Christians go about being distinctive in the wrong way, and why?

PLAY THE TRACK > > > > >

Play spot-the-difference. Divide the group into several smaller clusters and give one of the following scenarios to each. They must decide what being distinctive means in that situation and then act out their own ending to the whole group.

1. You are on a train with some non-Christian friends. A younger lad is sitting in the same carriage. Some youths get on and start being aggressive to him and demanding money. Your friends assume the best thing is not to get involved. You remember the story of the good Samaritan. How does the story unfold?

2. You are a trainee carpenter. You and your boss are fitting a kitchen. The fridge arrives and you unwrap it. It's the wrong size but you know now it's been taken out of its packaging you can't return it. Your boss is angry but says they will take it back if it's damaged. He dents the side with a block of timber and asks you to call them and tell them it's damaged and needs returning. How do you respond?

3. You are at a friend's party. Your best mate is not a Christian, but you know she is keen to know more and believes in God deep down. A good-looking boy invites her to go upstairs. You know this will not help in her exploration of God, but don't want to look like a killjoy. What do you do?

Allow each group to act out their sketch. Those watching must then identify who the Christian was in the sketch and how they were distinctive.

Ask these questions:

- How easy is it to be distinctive in real life situations?
- What do you need to help you do this?
- How can you avoid being weird, but still be distinctive in a way that makes sense to people?

Explain that you are going to do a quiz looking at some famous people and looking at the way they live their lives – the distinctive they have. Using the following list, name a person and suggest the group brainstorm what they know of them and how much these people stand – or stood – out or demonstrate their faith by their lifestyle:

- Britney Spears
- Mother Teresa
- Robbie Williams
- Princess Diana
- Tony Blair

Conclude the quiz by reading out Matthew 7:21. Say: 'It doesn't matter who we are or how famous we become. Everyone will stand shoulder to shoulder before God one day and the only thing that will count for anything is what we did or didn't do.'

End by asking for volunteers to read out Matthew 28:18-20, John 14:26 and John 16:13. Encourage them to ask God for inspiration on how to be distinctive in a way that doesn't seem weird – God is more creative than any of us will ever be.

Everyone will stand shoulder to shoulder before God one day

79. TV

TRACK 10: *Throw Away Your TV*

LENGTH: 3 mins 44 secs

IN BRIEF: This session deals with what is good and what is not good about TV. It helps people reflect on their own viewing and unpacks biblical guidelines for what we watch.

Album:
By The Way
(Warner, 2002)

Artist:
Red Hot Chilli Peppers

APPLICATION

Prior to this session, the leader should record clips from a variety of TV programmes that are popular with the group. As well as a TV and video you will need a variety of food stuffs laid out, ranging from the very sugary or fatty items such as chocolate, sweets and cream, through to more healthy things such as yoghurt, fruit and carrots.

Start by asking who agrees with the phrase 'You are what you eat', and why. Then ask who thinks there is a principle that you are influenced by things you consume, whether it is the music your ears consume, the food your mouth consumes or the TV programmes you eyes consume.

PLAY THE TRACK > > > > >

Play the track and ask the group what they think the message of the song is. You may get two different interpretations:

1. That TV is a 'plague' and that it is strangling ambition in people who watch too much of it. Getting rid of it will herald a fresh new chapter.

2. The song is, in fact, tongue in cheek about throwing your TV away. It's saying that the idea of chucking the TV to release ambition and grow as a person is naïve and one that's been round the block before.

Unpack both the interpretations above if they haven't been suggested. Ask who thinks TV does strangle ambition and who thinks that such ideas are old and outdated.

Read out Matthew 6:22-23 and ask:

■ What is Jesus saying in this passage?

■ How do you think you make your eyes 'good' or 'bad'?

Do the following quiz to help the group assess their own TV habits. Give out pens and paper and get each person to write their responses down:

1. After you have seen a TV programme that has impacted you in some way, how often does it come up in your mind again?

   (a) Once
   (b) Twice
   (c) More than five times

2. What is the earliest TV programme you can remember watching? How many years ago did you see it?

3. What genre of programmes affect you most:

   (a) The news
   (b) Documentaries
   (c) Nature programmes
   (d) Dramas
   (e) Lifestyle or fashion shows
   (f) Comedy
   (g) Other

4. What is your favourite programme?

5. How many hours of TV do you watch a week?

6. Have you ever fasted from TV? What effect did it have?

7. What would you say was the most unhelpful thing you have ever watched?

8. What do you think is worse on TV: sex, swearing and bad language, or violence?

9. In what ways does TV affect you?

Go through their answers and draw out people's responses. Use these as discussion starters.

Have the TV and video near to the food you have laid out. Show the clips you recorded, one by one. In between each clip, ask people which of the foodstuffs they think the programme compares to. For a show with lots of swearing and sex scenes, they might choose chocolate to indicate that though tasty, it rots the mind. Be sure to include a range of programmes – some good and some less so.

End by reading Philippians 4:8. Have some pieces of folded card that will stand up on their own. Ask the group to write the verse on the cards and challenge them to put them on top of their TVs.

You may also wish to suggest a group TV fast for a week.

80. THE CROSS

TRACK 8: I Could Die For You

LENGTH: 3 mins 13 secs

IN BRIEF: A chance to look at what the Cross means for us.

Album:
By The Way
(Warner, 2002)

Artist:
Red Hot Chilli Peppers

APPLICATION

Introduce the theme by reading the following:

> *The cross was used as a tool of execution for military and political criminals during Roman times. The victim was often made to carry the crossbeam to the execution site, where the vertical post was already fastened into the ground. They would then be nailed naked to the crossbeam, which was hoisted up and attached to the vertical beam. The pain was horrific and death was usually caused by suffocation. In the Old Testament, anybody put on a cross was considered cursed by God.*

Invite volunteers to read out Deuteronomy 21:22-23 and Isaiah 53:4-5.

PLAY THE TRACK > > > > >

Play the track and ask the group to make a note of any parts of the song that could apply to Jesus' death.

Have a flip chart or OHP. Draw two columns, labelling one, **'What You Get Free in Life'** and the second, **'What You Pay For in Life'**. Brainstorm ideas, whether material, spiritual or emotional.

Ask the question: 'Is the Cross of Christ for free?'

Allow for feedback, then split the group into two. Give the first Romans 3:21-31 and tell them to prepare arguments as to why the Cross of Christ is a free gift. The second group must look at James 2:14-26 and prepare arguments for why the Cross comes with expectations and involves a cost on our part.

Give each side 15 minutes to prepare, and then let them present their arguments.

Explain that both of these arguments are valid. They are different sides of the same coin. The Cross gives us new life – as a gift – through faith. However, faith will express itself in real actions.

Play the balloon game. Explain that you are all in a hot-air balloon that is crashing to earth. To save it from crashing, only two people can remain in it – the rest must jump out. Each person must come up with three reasons why they should be allowed to stay in the balloon and explain their reasons to the group. Appoint two people as judges to decide which two are most convincing and can stay.

Reflect on the game. Most people probably named things they had done as reasons why they deserved to stay. Explain that at heaven's gate God will not look at what we did to decide whether we can enter. He will look at whether we have faith in Jesus' death. However, he will know if we have real faith by whether it was expressed in our actions.

End by reading out two Bible passages that express both sides of this: Romans 5:6-8 and Matthew 25:41-43.

Give each person a penny to take away as a reminder that there are two sides to this coin.

God will know if we have real faith by whether it was expressed in our actions

81. POTENTIAL

TRACK 2: Feel

LENGTH: 4 mins 22 secs

IN BRIEF: This session deals with the potential God has put within each of us and the potential we have to use, or to waste these abilities.

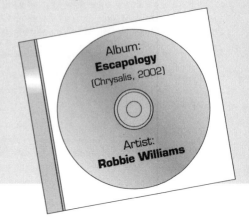

Album:
Escapology
(Chrysalis, 2002)

Artist:
Robbie Williams

APPLICATION

PLAY THE TRACK > > > > >

Start by playing the track.

Ask who feels as if they have 'too much life running through their veins going to waste'?

Split the group into three teams. Give each team 5 minutes to come up with the first part of a scenario relating to an imaginary person of their own age. The scenario must lead up to a crossroads which they reach in their life. The choice they face should be between doing the right thing and the wrong thing. The story must pause at the point where the person has a choice. Give this example to get them going:

> *Shelly is 19. She lives on an estate in Edinburgh. Her boyfriend, Mike, has asked her to marry him. She knows he makes his money through breaking into cars and flogging what he steals. She likes Mike a lot, but fears that marrying him would be the start of a slippery slope into crime for her. She has an offer from an Aunt in Glasgow to go and do an apprenticeship at her bakery. This would mean leaving Mike. What will she do?*

When they have done this, each team passes their scenario to the next team who then has another 10 minutes to end the story and come up with two scenarios, one in which the person chooses the wise route and the other in which the person goes down a bad route. The teams must come up with an ending to each scenario reflecting how things pan out in each case.

Ask each team to read out the story and their two endings and allow time for feedback and discussion.

Summarise the stories of Joseph and Judas for the group as examples of people who used their potential (Joseph: Genesis 39 and 41:39-57) and who didn't (Judas: Matthew 10:2-4, Matthew 26:14-16 and Matthew 27:3-5)

Ask the group for comments and ideas on how to know whether you are using or wasting your potential.

Explain that one way we can be certain that we use all the life God has put in our veins is to make sure we do the things that spark us and make us feel alive.

Prior to the meeting, prepare a sheet of paper with a wide range of activities written on, ranging from rock climbing, skateboarding and partying to reading, writing and helping people. Photocopy the sheet so that there are enough for one per person and cut the sheets into slips so that each activity is on a single slip.

Give out a set of slips of paper to each person. Instruct them to find the thing that they think most makes them come alive. They can write their own if their 'thing' is not in the pile.

Go round the room and invite each person to share what they chose and how they think they might be able to use that skill/favoured activity for God. Invite the rest of the group to throw in ideas for each person.

As each person shares their activity, write it on an OHP. When everyone's is listed, draw a circle around the words and then draw an arrow to another box in which you should write **'How can I use this for God?'** Draw a further arrow from that box to a final one in which you should write, **'What can I do to make that happen?'**

Encourage them to spend 5 minutes answering these questions relating to their activity – and to remember these questions as key ones to ask about all activities in their life to ensure they utilise their potential for God.

Play the track for a final time. Read out the verse about 'a hole in my soul' and close by emphasising to the group that it's when we do the things that God has made us good at, and gear them towards him that we fill the holes in our souls.

One way we can be certain that we use all the life God has put in our veins is to make sure we do the things that spark us and make us feel alive

82. HEAVEN AND HELL

TRACK 14: Nan's Song

LENGTH: 3 mins 52 secs

IN BRIEF: This session looks at what heaven is like, and at the reality of hell. It invites people to reflect on their own understanding of heaven.

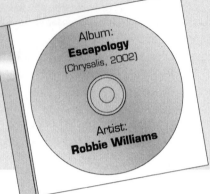

Album:
Escapology
(Chrysalis, 2002)

Artist:
Robbie Williams

APPLICATION

Set the scene for a session on heaven by dimming the lights or using lamps, playing ambient music and lighting candles around the room. Invite everyone to get comfortable, then read out the following verses relating to heaven:

Luke 10:20; Philippians 3:20; Revelation 5:13-14; Revelation 11:19; Revelation 19:1; Revelation 19:11-16.

PLAY THE TRACK > > > > >

Invite them to get comfortable and imagine what heaven is like as the track plays.

Have a big white sheet laid out (with some polythene between it and the floor to prevent stains) and invite everyone to draw on it, using paints or marker pens, their impression of heaven. Play the track again as they do that.

PLAY THE TRACK AGAIN > > > > >

Invite people to explain what they have drawn.

Do a short Bible study looking at what heaven is like. Use the following to help unpack the subject:

- ■ Heaven is where God dwells (Revelation 12:7-8). Heaven is therefore defined by God's presence.
- ■ Heaven is for the future (John 14:2). However, it is also with us now as we live for God (John 14:23).
- ■ At the end of time, there will be a new heaven and a new earth (Isaiah 65:17-19). This will happen at the second coming (2 Peter 3:10).
- ■ Those who follow Christ will spend eternity with him in heaven (John 3:16).

PLAY THE TRACK AGAIN > > > > >

This time tell the group to focus on the references to 'Nan', who has died. There are two sides to every coin, and this may be an appropriate time to talk about the reality of hell. Unpack the subject using these verses:

- ■ Hell is total separation from God and all that he represents. However, it is more than that – it is a real place (Matthew 5:30).
- ■ Hell is a place of torment (Luke 16:23).
- ■ God is the final judge of our eternal destiny (Luke 12:5).
- ■ In the parable of the sheep and goats, Jesus taught that he looks at how we live out his message to know whether it was real in us – and to know if we will spend eternity with him (Matthew 25:31-46).
- ■ Paul taught that those who never hear the gospel will be judged on how they responded to conscience and creation (Romans 1:18-20).

Hell is total separation from God and all that he represents

83. JOY AND PAIN

TRACK 11: Joy and Pain

LENGTH: 3 mins 47 secs

IN BRIEF: To understand that joy and pain are normal parts of every friendship and relationship.

Album:
Destination
(Polydor, 2001)

Artist:
Ronan Keating

APPLICATION

Start by looking at the opposite relationships that exist: light and dark, hot and cold, summer and winter, joy and pain. Explain that these work together so that on a cold winter's night, the heat of a fire seems all the more inviting. When you have experienced pain and it disappears, there is joy that the pain has gone. Or, when you are joyful or pleased about something, the emotion is sweeter because we know pain also exists.

PLAY THE TRACK > > > > >

Have an open discussion. Invite the group to shout out some of the things that bring them joy and pain in relationships.

Split the group into two smaller groups (or three if you have a large group). Explain you are going to play a game in which they have to be the first team to guess all the words on the leader's list. The words reflect either something joyful or painful about friendships and relationships.

Give each team a lump of play-dough. (An easy recipe for play-dough is: 2 cups of water, 2 teaspoons of cream of tartar, 4 drops of food colouring, 2 tablespoons of oil, 1 cup of salt, 2 cups of flour. Mix the ingredients together in a saucepan on a gentle heat. When it has a gooey consistency, it is ready. Do not overheat it or it will become too hard to use.)

Members of each team take turns to run to the leader who tells them one word from the following lists – and says which list it is from. The runner must then illustrate the word using the play-dough. They must not write the word in the dough, it must be guessed through a design they make with the dough. Once the guessers have discovered the word, they must also say whether it reflects a joy or pain in a relationship before the next runner can go to the leader.

WORDS:

JOY: presents, holidays, visiting the cinema, helping each other.

PAIN: arguments, splitting up, forgetting a birthday, saying sorry.

Explain that all relationships ebb and flow and that you're going to look at some relationships in the Bible which had their joys and pains. Either give the following passages to smaller groups to look at and report back on, or study them as one group. Bear these questions in mind as you read:

- What caused the pain in this situation?

- Was there an answer to, or way through the pain?

- Where was God during the pain?

- Can you see joy in this situation?

PETER AND JESUS:

Peter denies Jesus. John 18:15-18
Jesus reinstates Peter: John 21:15-17

JESUS AND HIS FATHER:

Luke 22:39-44: Jesus struggles to accept the pain ahead of him
Mark 15:33-34: Jesus feels the pain of separation from God.

MARY AND MARTHA:

John 10:17-37: the pain of Mary, Martha and the Jews
John 10:38-44: the joy of Lazarus being raised.

JOB:

Job 1:1-5: Job enjoys wealth, family and relationship with God
Job 19:1-11: Job rebukes his friends for their lack of comfort and feels the pain of feeling God is against him.

Draw to a close by allowing time for the group to pray and to offer their current joys and pains to God.

When you are joyful, the emotion is sweeter because we know pain also exists

84. BEFORE IT'S TOO LATE

TRACK 3: If Tomorrow Never Comes

LENGTH: 3 mins 34 secs

IN BRIEF: To look at how well we communicate our love to those we are close to. Song lyrics available at www.ronankeating.com

Album:
Destination
(Polydor, 2001)

Artist:
Ronan Keating

Note: You will need to be very aware of anyone in the group who has lost someone close to them.

APPLICATION

Start by asking everyone in the group to think of someone they love very much. Then give them a few minutes to write some of the things they would say about them if they unexpectedly died and they had to do a speech at their funeral. Include the following:

- What their best characteristic was.
- Why you enjoyed being with them.
- What your favourite memory with them was.
- What their sense of humour was like.

Tell them this is just for them – they will not be asked to share what they write.

Explain that you are not trying to be morbid. However, in the West, there is often an aversion to thinking about death and separation until we are forced to. This meeting is an opportunity to consider these things before it is too late.

PLAY THE TRACK > > > > >

Ask them whether, if they didn't wake up tomorrow, the person they wrote about would know how much they loved them, what they enjoyed most about them and why they meant so much to them?

Give out paper, pens and envelopes and ask them to write a letter to this person telling them how much they appreciate them. It doesn't have to be slushy, just honest. They can either post it to them, or just keep it as a reminder of what they want to say to the person.

PLAY THE TRACK AGAIN > > > > >

Give them 10 minutes – or longer if required – to write their letters, while the track is playing.

Give out Bibles and turn to 1 Samuel 20:16-17 and 41-42. Explain that David was to be the future king of Israel and made the current king – Saul – feel insecure. Jonathan was Saul's son and David and Jonathan had a deep friendship. Despite David's concern that he would soon die, Jonathan in fact died only a short time later. Read 2 Samuel 1:25-27 where David mourns for Jonathan.

Explain that David and Jonathan had an honest and deep friendship. When they saw each other for the last time, they expressed their love for each other (1 Samuel 20:41-42) even though they expected to meet again. They took the opportunity.

End by playing the encouragement game. Ask everyone to write their name at the bottom of a piece of clean paper. They then pass their paper to the person on their left who has 3 minutes to write something they like about the person whose name is at the foot of the page. They then fold the top over to hide what they have written, and everyone passes the paper to the left to repeat the exercise. When the paper has gone full circle and returns to the person whose name is on it, everyone can unravel their own bits and read the encouragements.

In the West, there is often an aversion to thinking about death and separation until we are forced to

85. HEARTBEAT OF GOD

TRACK 1: Breathe Your Name

LENGTH: 3 mins 50 secs

IN BRIEF: A chance to explore how we recognise the heartbeat and voice of God within us.

Album:
Divine Discontent
(Reprise, 2002)

Artist:
Sixpence None the Richer

APPLICATION

Read John 16:13 from a contemporary translation.

Carry out this mini-survey to stimulate the group's thinking about the idea of God's presence within. Ask people to raise their hands and explain their answers:

1. I'm most aware of God within me when I'm (a) terrified (b) happy (c) struggling (d) in church (e) with friends (f) praying (g) outside in the open air.

2. I know God is with me because I (a) feel him in some way (b) have been told he is since I was a kid (c) think he's with everyone all the time (d) talk to him and know he's there.

3. If God suddenly left and wasn't in or around me I'd feel (a) totally empty and lost (b) pretty much the same (c) different, but unable to pinpoint why (d) disappointed, but OK.

4. I see most evidence that God is real through (a) nature and creation (b) other people who follow Jesus (c) my own experience of God (d) people who trust God through very difficult situations in their lives.

Use question 3 as a discussion starter: How would the world and our lives change if God removed himself?

Introduce the track. Explain that it raises the question of whether God's presence is all just a figment of imagination, 'inside my head'.

PLAY THE TRACK > > > > >

Start the track. At 2 minutes 14 seconds into the song, there is an instrumental. During this read John 14:16-17.

When the track has finished re-read John 14:16-17 and explain that you are going to take God at his word and spend 5 minutes listening for God's voice.

Encourage them to keep their thoughts on God and to be expectant that he will draw near. Emphasise, however, that they shouldn't expect some huge revelation. In 1 Kings 19:12-13, God appears to Elijah in a whisper, not in an earthquake or fire. Read this as preparation.

Raise their expectations that God will speak to them in a way unique to them. It may be helpful to mention the following as ways God may reveal himself to them: through a thought or word which keeps bouncing into their minds; through a sense of peace; through a feeling of warmth; through a picture in their minds; through a Bible verse; through a recollection of something someone said to them; through some other way particular to them. Playing some music while the group are silent may help reduce the potential for awkwardness or embarrassment.

After the silence, encourage people to feed back, however silly they might feel their comments are. Be sure to encourage anyone who does speak up. For those who feel God didn't 'meet' them, remind them of Elijah in 1 Kings 19 – that he had to learn to distinguish God's voice from the distractions of wind, fire and earthquake. Encourage them to practice the discipline of waiting and listening.

Sum up by referring back to the song – that when everything seems to be falling apart, Christians can still 'breathe God's name' and know he is with them.

End with this benediction:

Leave in the knowledge that Christ is closer to you than the hair on your head and the skin on your hands.

Leave knowing that Christ is close by – with a commitment stronger than iron and a love broader than space.

Make time to respond to Christ's love daily. Let him speak to you. Make space in your heart to hear his direction, affirmation and friendship. Talk to him knowing he listens to you.

Breathe his name daily and take time to hear his heartbeat of love for you.

Leave with the blessing and presence of God the Father, God the Son and God the Holy Spirit within you.

86. UNANSWERED QUESTIONS

TRACK 5: Waiting on the Sun

LENGTH: 2 mins 50 secs

IN BRIEF: A chance to explore what it means to live life with unanswered questions and incomplete knowledge. An exploration of Paul's unanswered prayer.

Album:
Divine Discontent
(Reprise, 2002)

Artist:
Sixpence None the Richer

APPLICATION

Explain to the group that the track is about accepting our incompleteness – this could relate to anything from our faith to our future. The track advocates living with the tension of having unanswered questions, seeing weakness as a strength and being willing to accept our doubts rather than letting them trip us up.

PLAY THE TRACK > > > > >

The track is about accepting our incompleteness

Read 2 Corinthians 12:7-10. Split the group into smaller clusters and give these questions, and Bibles, out for them to discuss:

■ How many times did Paul 'plead with God' before he decided to simply live with his request unanswered? What does this say about the idea that real Christians have all questions relating to their faith answered and no loose ends left hanging?

■ Why do you think God told Paul that 'my power is made perfect in weakness'? Are there times this has been true in your life?

■ How do you feel about the idea that God was the one who allowed Paul to live with 'a thorn in the flesh', 'a messenger of Satan'? Does this change the way you look at things that are hard to cope with in life?

Divide the group into pairs. Invite them to share with their partner any areas they feel incomplete in, or in which they have asked for God's solution but have not had an answer. Suggest each pair pray for one another, using 2 Corinthians 12:8-9 as a stimulus.

Close by encouraging the group to see any areas they struggle in or questions they have as chances to be 'made perfect in weakness'.

Can we live with the tension of having unanswered questions, see weakness as a strength and be willing to accept our doubts rather than letting them trip us up?

87. PASSION FOR GOD

TRACK 3: Consuming Fire

LENGTH: 6 mins 35 secs

IN BRIEF: This session uses fire as a means for exploring and understanding the passion God wants to stir up in his people.

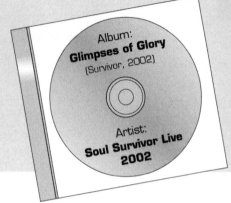

Album:
Glimpses of Glory
(Survivor, 2002)

Artist:
Soul Survivor Live 2002

APPLICATION

This track would work well being used as part of a meeting held round a bonfire. Obviously this requires consideration to be given to safety. However, if an outdoor venue is available the fire provides a powerful visual illustration. This would also work well on a residential or camp.

Start by explaining that fire was often used by God as a symbol of his presence. This included:

- God appeared to Moses in a burning bush (Exodus 3:2).
- God guided Israel in a pillar of fire (Exodus 13:21).
- The fire on the Lord's altar was to be kept always burning (Leviticus 6:12).
- God's fire came out and consumed the people's burnt offerings (Leviticus 9:24).
- The fire of God burnt up the offering Elijah had prepared (1 Kings 18:38).
- Elijah was taken to heaven in a chariot of fire (2 Kings 2:11).
- The Holy Spirit came in tongues of fire at Pentecost (Acts 2:3).

When the fire is lit, invite the group to think about and to throw ideas in as to how fire is symbolic of God. Suggestions might include:

- Fire purifies.
- Fire cannot be touched by human hands.
- Fire is wild and when it gets a hold, it changes the thing it catches (purifies it).
- Fire can destroy even the strongest tree. Nothing can stand in its way.

Then ask them to think about how fire is like the Christian life. Suggestions might include:

- Fire needs feeding if it is to grow.
- Calm conditions do not make the fire grow – rough weather does.
- Those who come near fire know they have been close to it.
- One fire can start hundreds of other fires.

Calm the group and read Malachi 3:2-3 from the NCV translation: *'He will be like purifying fire . . . Like someone who heats and purifies silver, he will purify the [people] and make them pure like gold and silver.'*

Tell the group that you are going to start the track. Invite them, as you do, to let God speak to them through the visual aid of the fire. You could get them to spend a few minutes, in silence, listening to the fire crackling and welcoming God to come and work in their hearts as they listen to the track and watch the fire.

PLAY THE TRACK > > > > >

After the track has finished, give out sheets of blank paper.

Explain that in the same way that the heat of the fire purifies gold and silver, the heat of God's Holy Spirit purifies us. On the sheet of paper write or draw anything you think God wants to burn up in your life. It could be an attitude, a habit, a magazine you read or a TV programme you watch.

When you have written this down, offer it to God to burn up in you, and screw up the paper and throw it in the fire.

As the group does this, lead them in a prayer, asking for God to strengthen their resolve to see these things burnt up in them. Then lead them in a prayer reflecting the words of the track that God would fan into flame a passion for his name.

PLAY THE TRACK AGAIN > > > > >

As you play the track again, invite the group to express their desire to God for him to fan into flame their passion again.

Close by reading out Romans 12:11. Give it out on slips of paper for the group to take away.

88. BOWING DOWN

TRACK 9: As Angels Looked On

LENGTH: 4 mins 38 secs

IN BRIEF: An opportunity to consider the role our bodies can have in worshipping God.

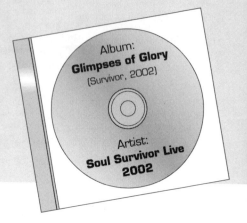

Album:
Glimpses of Glory
(Survivor, 2002)

Artist:
Soul Survivor Live 2002

APPLICATION

It can be easy to get so wrapped up in asking God for his help and mercy, that we forget we have something to give back to him: ourselves.

This track is about bowing down in the face of Jesus' overwhelming love for us. Try to avoid making it more complicated than that. Keep this session simple and resist the temptation to cover other bases.

Pick out several volunteers. Give one of the following emotions words to each person:

ANGRY   FED-UP   JOYFUL   BORED   EXCITED   TIRED

Instruct them, one by one, to act out their word without speaking. When the rest of the group have guessed the words, ask them to think about how they guessed the feelings they were acting out. Explain that we use our bodies as a second mouth. We communicate to people as much by how we posture our bodies as by what we actually say.

Ask who uses their body in worship and in what ways? Why do they find that helpful?

Give out these verses to members of the group to read aloud:

- Psalm 5:7
- Psalm 95:6
- Psalm 138:2
- Isaiah 45:22-23
- Philippians 2:10-11

After each verse is read, invite people to comment on why they think emphasis is being put upon the role of the body in expressing the feelings of the heart. Are words not enough?

Say that throughout the Bible, God calls his followers to express their devotion through their physical worship as much as their verbal worship. In Mark 12:30, Jesus calls people to follow with their hearts, souls, minds AND strength – to make it a holistic act.

When people bow before something they are demonstrating their willingness to be vulnerable and are showing they trust whatever it is they are bowing before. After all, they would be defenceless in the face of attack while on their knees. Bowing down shows a willingness to trust and give the whole person over.

Over 70 per cent of communication is non-verbal. We communicate more about how we feel by what we do with our bodies than what we say with our mouths. We are going to use our bodies to express what we feel in our hearts about God.

PLAY THE TRACK > > > > >

Read one or two of the verses as the track starts and invite the group to express their love for God by kneeling or bowing before God.

A physical action can be a prayer to God. Encourage them to consider using their bodies to express their prayers to God at home.

Throughout the Bible, God calls his followers to express their devotion through their physical worship as much as their verbal worship

89. THE OPEN ARMS OF GOD

TRACK 8: *Open Arms — The Prodigal*

LENGTH: *6 mins 13 secs*

IN BRIEF: *A look at the story of the prodigal son, applying the story's lessons to our experience with God today.*

Album:
Making Your Mark
(ICC, 2002)

Artist:
The Summer Madness Band

APPLICATION

Explain that the session is about the prodigal son and provide a brief outline of the story. Ask the group, as they listen to the track, to write down the different emotions and questions that the prodigal son, the brother and the father, display. Have three different pieces of fruit visible to represent the three characters: a bruised and worn banana (the prodigal son); a bitter lemon (the brother); a big shiny red apple (the father).

PLAY THE TRACK > > > > >

Allow people to feed back what they wrote down. Ask each person to consider which of the characters they most closely represent in their current situations.

The rest of the session is a reading of the story from *The Message* with questions and application inserted for the group to consider the teaching of the account for them. If a copy of *The Message* is not available, use an NIV and slot in the sections below at the indicated verse.

THE LOST SON – LUKE 15:11-32.

Read the first part of the story down to the paragraph which ends: 'but no one would give him any' (verses 11-16 in NIV). At this point read the following, slowly:

> *Have you ever thrown off things which seemed to be holding you back from becoming who you wanted to be?*
>
> *Have you ever indulged your appetite for a good time only to get an empty, sinking feeling?*
>
> *The Bible says: 'Be happy while you are young . . . Remember your Creator while you are young' (Ecclesiastes 11 and 12).*

How are you living the life God has leased to you?

Listen to your breathing. Feel your pulse. The life God has put in you surges through you.

God expects you to use this life and, like the prodigal, to take risks.

But he wants you to know that life can only be lived to the full with him at the centre.

Read the Bible story down to the paragraph which ends: 'and went home to his father' (verses 17-20 in NIV). Then read the following, slowly:

Why did the Son go home? Was he sorry he'd wasted his father's wealth or that he'd insulted and dishonoured the family name?

No way. If he'd found some more money, his father wouldn't have seen him for dust.

It was his stomach talking sense, not his heart repenting.

Be honest about what drives you to seek God. Is it the warm feeling of his presence? Is it the need to know he's guiding you? Is it the situation that's worrying you that you want to give to him? Or, is it that he's your father and, as his child, you belong with him?

Spend a few minutes thinking about the reasons you are drawn to God.

Read the Bible story down to the paragraph which ends: 'they began to have a wonderful time' (verses 21-24). Then read the following slowly:

Did the father ask about the son's motives for returning? No. His welcome was unconditional.

What changed the son's heart? Probably the overwhelming love of the father.

The father represents God. He will welcome us whatever our motives for seeking him.

God gives us free choice in how we use the many abilities he gives us.

When we act like the prodigal, he waits for us to return.

Do you feel God calling you to return to him? He will welcome you like he welcomed the son in the story.

Read the Bible story down to the paragraph which ends: 'go all out with a feast' (verses 25-30 in NIV). Then read the following, slowly:

Have you ever watched someone live it up for years while you quietly and faithfully served God?

When they decided to turn to God and there were bells and whistles, and the modern-day fatted calf was slaughtered to celebrate, was there a twinge of jealousy?

Most of us would feel jealous.

However, God sees the full picture and we only see half.

We must bring any jealousy at how God seems to bless others to him and let him show us the full picture. God sees it differently . . .

Read the final paragraph of the story from the Bible, then read the following, slowly:

The lavishness shown to the prodigal didn't affect or detract from the love the father had for his other son.

It comes back to our motives for following God. If our motive is that he is our father and we want to be close to him – and not because we crave what he gives us – then jealousy will evaporate with the father's words: 'Everything I have is yours and you are with me all the time'.

90. WORSHIP

TRACK 4: Here I Am to Worship

LENGTH: 6 mins 30 secs

IN BRIEF: A look at the breadth of what worship is in the Bible and what it means in daily life.

Album:
Making Your Mark
(ICC, 2002)

Artist:
The Summer Madness Band

APPLICATION

PLAY THE TRACK > > > > >

Ask the group to brainstorm what worship is and come up with a definition.

Get some people to read the following and others to make notes of what each verse says about worship:

- 2 Chronicles 5:13-14 (God meets us when we worship).
- Acts 4:31 (God sends his Spirit when we worship).
- Acts 2:46-47 (worship can be evangelistic and can drive us to evangelism).
- John 4:21-24 (worship is a heart attitude).
- Isaiah 58:6-12 (worship is helping others and bringing justice in society).
- Psalm 100 (worship is a way to express all God has given us).

Worship is a way to express all God has given us

Allow the people who made notes to feed back. Identify key words from their feedback which reflect the characteristics of worship. Ensure they reflect the breadth of what worship is. Write these on a flipchart or OHP.

Give out paper. Instruct the group to draw a line down the centre. In the left column, they should write three activities they will do during the next week. They could be anything from ballet classes to cinema. In the other column, they should write down what it will mean for them to worship God in those activities, based on the words defining worship, above.

PLAY THE TRACK AGAIN > > > > >

Tell them to think about worship in its broadest sense as they listen and to make it personal. How will they worship God in all their experiences this week?

Worship is helping others and bringing justice in society

91. SPIRITUAL JOURNEY

TRACKS 16 AND 17: Little Journey & Live at Dominoes

LENGTH: 7 mins 15 secs in total

IN BRIEF: This session gets young people to draw a spiritual time line of their lives and assess their own spiritual development.

Album:
Since I Left You
(Modular, 2000)

Artist:
The Avalanches

APPLICATION

Start by playing 'What's the Time Mr Wolf?' Select a volunteer to face the wall. They must turn round quickly at intermittent intervals to face the rest of the group. The rest of the group must start from the opposite end of the room and sneak up on them. When s/he turns round, any who are not completely still are out. The winner is the one who can touch the back of the person facing the wall without being seen moving on their journey.

After the game say: 'Some journeys are quick, some are slow. Some require skill to walk them; others happen without us realising we are on them. During this session, we are going to look at spiritual journeys.'

Explain that you are going to call out a type of journey and you want the group to shout out words to describe that journey. For example, if you say 'hill walking' they might respond with anything from 'exhilarating' to 'demanding'. Use the following list of journeys:

- A journey in a hot, sticky car
- Your journey through childhood
- A journey to a holiday by the sea with friends
- The journey through teenage years
- A 12-hour plane journey
- Your journey with God

Explain that you are going to listen to a track around the theme of journey. Give them several minutes to think through their own spiritual journey and encourage them as they listen to consider the question: How far have I come on my journey with God?

The track – 'Little Journey' – depicts someone journeying through different environments. Allow it to roll into track 17.

PLAY THE TRACKS > > > > >

Unpack the idea of a spiritual time-line – a diagram that plots the key milestones or experiences in a person's life which have affected their relationship with God. Tell them they are going to draw spiritual time-lines for their own lives, charting how they have developed in their relationship with God.

Suggest that they split their lives into two-year blocks, trying to identify in those time frames any significant things that happened. They should include both 'spiritual' events (baptism) and 'secular' events (D of E Award) and try to identify what all their experiences have meant for their relationship with God. They should include good things as well as bad and also the time before they were Christians – to identify ways God might have been waking them up spiritually.

PLAY THE TRACKS AGAIN > > > > >

Play the tracks again as a background and give them 15 minutes to draw their spiritual time-line on paper. Invite people to explain their time-line to the rest of the group.

End by suggesting that they write under their time-lines any thoughts they have about how they want to develop spiritually in the next two years and what they will need to do to achieve this.

How far have I come on my journey with God?

92. TRUANCY

TRACK 13: Frontier Psychiatrist

LENGTH: 4 mins 46 secs

IN BRIEF: A look at why young people play truant and at how Jesus responded to people who couldn't cope.

Album:
Since I Left You
(Modular, 2000)

Artist:
The Avalanches

APPLICATION

Start by throwing out the following questions and allowing time for an open brainstorm:

- What are some common reasons why young people play truant?
- What are some common responses teachers and parents make to truancy?
- In your experience, have those dealing with truants looked beyond the act itself to discover the deeper causes?
- Is expulsion a good solution to truancy?

PLAY THE TRACK > > > > >

Ask the group to make a note of any labels or words used to describe Declan – the lad who is playing truant – in the song.

Split the group into two and give one of the following scenarios to each along with the instructions:

Jesus did not label those he met; he re-labelled them

SCENARIO 1

Jenny had always been lippy to teachers and other pupils. There were rumours that her Dad was in prison, no one ever saw her Mum. Her older sister would come to parents' evenings with her. It was during her mock GCSEs that her attendance became erratic. Her teachers could not discover why and had to threaten her with detentions and possible suspension.

■ If you were one of Jenny's teachers, how might you deal with her?

■ As a group, come up with the scenario for the part of Jenny's life no one sees – her home life.

SCENARIO 2

Peter was from a wealthy family. He had never fitted in well at school. Other pupils made constant jabs about his posh accent and his obsession with getting into Oxford University. His parents put loads of pressure on him, and as his A levels approached, he began to be absent without reason. The rumour was that he was at the library revising. His parents were called in and Peter was threatened with expulsion.

■ Would you have much sympathy for Peter if he was at your school?

■ As a group, come up with the scenario for the part of Peter's life no one sees – his home life.

Ask a volunteer to read out Matthew 9:9-13. Raise these points/questions:

■ If Jesus came to your school, who would he want to meet first? The pupils at the top of the class or those like Jenny and Peter who were struggling to cope?

■ What does Jesus mean by, 'I desire mercy, not sacrifice'? (v.13)

■ Jesus described himself here as a doctor. As his disciples, what does this say about our role with people who are struggling?

Invite the group to feed back any words or labels they made a note of when listening to the song. Explain that it is very easy to label people, particularly those who are different in some way. Jesus did not label those he met; he re-labelled them.

Staying as one group, ask a volunteer to read out the account of Jesus and Zacchaeus in Luke 19:1-10. Follow it up with the questions:

■ Zacchaeus was labelled a 'sinner' by those around him (v.7). What was Jesus saying about that label by going to his house?

■ What effect did Jesus' actions have on Zacchaeus? What does this say about what motivates people to change their ways?

■ Do you put labels on people? Why?

■ What effect does negative labelling have on people? What is Jesus saying here about negative labelling?

93. SIN

TRACK 9: Never Lose the Wonder

LENGTH: 4 mins 50 secs

IN BRIEF: This session brings to life the reality of sin and the power of Jesus to deal with it.

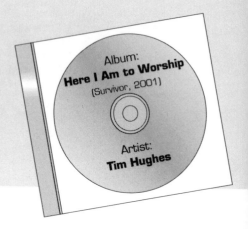

Album:
Here I Am to Worship
(Survivor, 2001)

Artist:
Tim Hughes

APPLICATION

PLAY THE TRACK > > > > >

Divide those present into groups of three. Instruct them to read Isaiah 53:4-12 and then mark a line down the centre of a sheet of paper labelling one column 'The Wonder of Jesus' Death' and the second, 'The Cost for Jesus'. Allow them 10 minutes to fill in the columns from what is written in the passage.

When they have done this, allow each group to feed back. Then raise these questions:

■ The cost for Jesus was significant. This reflects the depth of his love for the human race. How does it make you feel that someone loved you enough to die for you?

■ The cross was all about us being able to re-connect with God. Do you feel that you experience the joy of being connected with God every (a) day (b) week (c) month (d) year (e) never?

■ The need for Jesus' death suggests our hearts are pretty sinful in their natural state. Do you feel like that's the case?

Before the meeting, make sure you have prepared several bowls of swampy mud from some garden earth and water, don't make them too watery – keep it thick. Label these 'Poison Which Kills'. Add some ice cubes to these before the meeting.

Also, prepare some bowls of warm, clean water. Label these 'Jesus' Blood – Removing the Poison'. Add some red food colouring to these. Place them all on a plastic sheet to prevent the floor getting messy.

Ask a few volunteers to line up next to the bowls of mud, ready to sink their hands in. Also, label a couple of other volunteers as 'The Holy Spirit' and instruct them to gently wash away the mud when the other volunteers place their hands in the 'Jesus' Blood' bowls. Start the track again and read the following, slowly:

> *Imagine this mud is what's in your hearts.*
>
> *Jesus said that out of each human heart comes evil thoughts, sexual immorality, theft, and much more. This mud represents the state of your heart when you have hated people around you, lied, shouted and lost control, lusted after people or possessions, inflicted pain on someone, refused to forgive or stolen from somebody.*
>
> *The scary thing is that it can't be reversed by anything you do, however good it may be. Once our actions and thoughts create the sin, it stays and it stains.*
>
> *Sink your hands into the mud. Like sin, it's cold, dark and suffocating. And like sin, it forms a barrier, blocking out God.*
>
> *Take your hands out and try to remove the mud from them using just your hands. (Wait while they try.)*
>
> *The mud is like sin. It sticks, and nothing we can do will remove it. It's like poison – it blocks us from Jesus and destroys our character.*
>
> *Sin is not insignificant. Jesus was punished for our sins and crushed for our iniquities. If he hadn't died on the cross, we wouldn't be able to get rid of the sin. Only his death removes our sin and brings us into contact with God.*
>
> *Now take your hands out of the mud and place them in the bowls labelled 'Jesus' Blood' but don't try and clean them or do anything more than place them there.*
>
> *The Holy Spirit is the one who removes the sin by placing it upon Jesus. In the passage you read earlier, it says that Jesus' punishment brings us peace.*

PLAY THE TRACK AGAIN > > > > >

To end, play the track again and encourage the group to thank God for his death. If there are people present who have not received God's forgiveness, this may be an opportunity to suggest it.

94. GIVING YOUR ALL

TRACK 2: May the Words of My Mouth

LENGTH: 4 mins 12 secs

IN BRIEF: A chance to consider what 'giving your all to God' means.

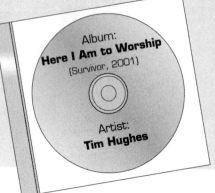

Album:
Here I Am to Worship
(Survivor, 2001)

Artist:
Tim Hughes

APPLICATION

This would fit well at a time when members of your group are on the edge of something big – a gap year or a new job. It's a song of commitment and so could also be used at the end of a residential or time away as a group.

Encourage the group to see it as a chance to reaffirm their commitment to giving their all to God.

Ask the group to think about a time when they gave their all to something, and in pairs to answer these questions:

- How would you define 'giving your all' to something?
- What made you want to give your all to that, at that time?
- How absorbing did the thing you were giving your all to become?
- What does giving your all to God mean for you?

PLAY THE TRACK > > > > >

As it finishes, and before people start moving, read the lyrics of the song from the CD inlay and explain that this is what commitment to God is about: surrendering and giving over to him our thoughts and our actions; committing to follow him; not seeking material treasures above him; and inviting him to give us a new vision and meaning for our lives.

Read out the following account of St Cuthbert, the English monk who lived around 1,350 years ago (died 687) and who made great sacrifices to pursue God and his purposes.

> Cuthbert was born in England more than 1,300 years ago. He met Jesus after having a vision involving heaven, and became a monk at Melrose in Scotland in 651 AD. He was an evangelist, and undertook dangerous journeys to minister to the poor. He lived with minimal material distractions and spent the last years of his life on the island of Inner Farne, Northumbria, ministering to those who visited him. He wrote, 'even if I could hide myself away in a tiny dwelling on a rock . . . not even there should I consider myself to be free from the snares of this deceptive world; but I should fear, lest the love of wealth might tempt me and somehow still snatch me away'.

Ask these questions:

- Can we really give our all to God when we are surrounded by so many attractive things?
- Should we shut ourselves away on an island, like St Cuthbert?
- What did Jesus' visit to earth teach about this?

PLAY THE TRACK AGAIN > > > > >

Close by playing the track again. Give out Psalm 19:14 (the verse the song is based on) on slips of paper.

95. FAITH FOR THE FUTURE

TRACK 5: Do You Know What Your Future Will Be?

LENGTH: 4 mins 23 secs

IN BRIEF: This session looks at the reality of faith and at our trust in God to be with us into the future.

Album:
Onka's Big Moka
(Sony, 2000)

Artist:
Toploader

APPLICATION

Give out pens and paper to the group. Instruct them to draw a matchstick person to represent themselves in the centre of the page, then to draw a circle the size of a mug around it. They should then draw a second, larger circle around the first one – about the size of a plate. There should be enough room to write in each circle. Finally, around the edge of the largest circle a bigger circle should be drawn – one that almost touches the outer edges of the page.

Give them 5 minutes to write in the smallest circle a list of the things in their future which they have some control over e.g. what kind of job they get, the person they marry. In the second, larger circle, they should write things about their future over which they will have no control e.g. terminal illness, job loss.

Allow people to feed back the kinds of things they have written in each circle, and how they feel about the things they will have no control over.

PLAY THE TRACK > > > > >

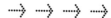

Play the track, then use the following lines from the song as discussion starters:

- Does the line 'keep faith on the shelf to use when you're not well' reflect how you see faith at times?
- 'Do you know what your future will be?' The answer to this is no. Does that worry you?

Explain that in this session we are looking at what our faith counts for when the rubber hits the road. When we are faced with a future in which good and bad things are bound to happen and over which we have little control, we need to connect with someone bigger than us, someone who knows our future.

Read out the second part of Matthew 5:45 where Jesus talks about the sun rising on the good and the evil. Emphasise that being a Christian does not mean we have a 'get out of jail free' card excluding us from difficulties in life.

Have a volunteer read out Romans 8:38-39 and make the point that nothing that happens to us in life can separate us from God.

Tell the group to find their pieces of paper with the circles on and to draw a line from the hand of the matchstick person to beyond the outer edge of the largest circle. They should then look up Psalm 62:8 and write this verse in the space between the largest circle and the outer edge of the page.

Explain that although some things in our future will be outside of our control, none of them are outside God's control – and we are connected to the One who sees all.

Tell the group that you are going to create a time capsule. In it, they can each place a letter to God detailing something they are worried about in the near future. Explain that as a group you will dig it up in a year's time and use it as a faith exercise – to look back on what they were worried about and see how God has helped them in that situation. Bury the time capsule somewhere where it will not be dug up by accident. Encourage the group to be honest – no one else will read what they have written. When you bury it, emphasise that God sees what they have written.

End by reading 2 Timothy 1:1-12. This is Paul's letter to Timothy when he was imprisoned under Nero (AD 66-67). He was in a cold dungeon, in chains. It offers an incredible insight into the Apostle's level of faith – despite his circumstances. Look particularly at verse 12.

96. THE HOLY SPIRIT

Album:
Onka's Big Moka
(Sony, 2000)

Artist:
Toploader

TRACK 8: High Flying Bird

LENGTH: 4 mins 10 secs

IN BRIEF: This session deals with the characteristics of the Holy Spirit and its role in our lives.

APPLICATION

Tell the group you are going to look at some of the characteristics of the Holy Spirit. Introduce the track and ask the group as they listen to try to identify similarities and differences between the bird in the song and the Holy Sprit.

PLAY THE TRACK > > > > >

During the first 50 seconds of music, before the lyrics start, read Romans 8:26-27.

Feed back similarities and differences the group noticed.

SIMILARITIES:

- It is described as a bird – Matthew 3:16
- It cannot be seen
- It is outside of time
- It recognises trouble on earth below

DIFFERENCES:

- The Holy Spirit comes down and gets involved in life on earth – he does not remain aloof

Split the group into three smaller teams. Give each team 10 minutes to share honestly among themselves areas in which they struggle to do the right thing. This could be anything from smoking to looking at magazines that are unhelpful, to picking on someone in school.

When they have done this, explain that you are going to do a group Bible Study on the characteristics of the Holy Spirit. Use the following as a guide:

- The Holy Spirit is the third person in the Trinity, bringing the Father and Son close to believers (John 14:16, John 14:26).
- Through his power we come to Christ and are forgiven and made new (John 3:6, John 6:63).
- The Holy Spirit is the helper Jesus promised (John 14:25-26).
- The Holy Spirit brings people to conviction of their sin (John 16:8).
- The Holy Spirit communicates what he hears from the Father and Son (John 15:26; 1 Corinthians 2:10-12).
- The Holy Spirit's main job is to promote the life and teaching of Jesus by making it a reality in believers' lives and actions (John 14:15-17).
- The Holy Spirit gives gifts to Jesus' followers to help them in their mission (1 Corinthians 12:4-27).

Invite the groups to think back to the things they shared in small groups that they struggled with. Explain that the Holy Spirit is so called because he helps us be Holy – he helps us choose right. Allow them to spend some time back in their small groups praying for each other – for the Holy Spirit's strength and help to choose right over wrong.

End by reading Joel 2:28-29 and praying for group members to receive a fresh empowering of the Holy Spirit.

The Holy Spirit is so called because he helps us be Holy – he helps us choose right

97. JUST BAD LUCK?

TRACK 7: Why Does it Always Rain on Me?

LENGTH: 4 mins 24 secs

IN BRIEF: A look at whether tough things we go through are punishments for bad things we have done.

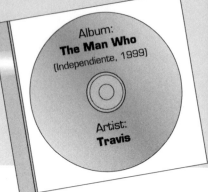

Album:
The Man Who
(Independiente, 1999)

Artist:
Travis

APPLICATION

Ask whether the group thinks that the difficult events and situations in their lives are:

- Pure chance?
- Organised and controlled by God?
- Some kind of retribution for things done wrong in the past?

PLAY THE TRACK > > > > >

Give out sheets of paper with four columns drawn on. Head the columns with the following words: **'Spitting', 'Drizzling', 'Pouring', 'Torrential Downpour'.**

Give them 5 minutes to think of as many situations as they can of when they went through difficult times and to write a word or two about each in the column they think it best fits ('spitting' being something annoying; 'torrential downpour' being failing your driving test for the sixth time).

When they have done this ask them to place a 1 or 2 by each situation on their paper to reflect what they think the reason was that these things happened to them. The numbers should relate to the following. Write these up somewhere visible:

1 = 'What goes around comes around'. Like the song said, this happened because 'I lied when I was 17' and in some weird way I brought it on myself.

2 = Difficult things happen to everyone, whoever they are. In this situation though, I think God helped me through it and minimised the situation to help me.

Encourage people to share some of their situations and the reasons they think they happened.

Ask: 'How do you react in difficult times?' Write each of the following reactions on a separate sheet of paper and lay one in each corner of the room:

- ■ Be a hermit. Take it out on myself.
- ■ Get aggressive with people. Take it out on others.
- ■ Try to lose myself and forget it by partying or going out.
- ■ Talk about it with God, friends or family.

Tell the group that you are going to read out a scenario of a difficult time and they have to go and stand in the place reflecting most closely how they think they would react. Tell them that they have only 3 seconds from when you read the scenario to make their choice and run and stand in the place. Include other scenarios to suit your group. Include these:

- ■ You fail your driving test for the third time – unfairly, you feel.
- ■ Your boy/girlfriend unexpectedly breaks up with you.
- ■ You have your heart set on a particular job. You get short-listed but at the final interview don't get it.
- ■ A close friend or family member dies.
- ■ Your parents split up

PLAY THE TRACK AGAIN > > > > >

Split the group into smaller clusters and play the track again. Give them Matthew 5:45 (the second half of the verse relating to the sun and rain) to read, along with Job 2:3-10 and Matthew 5:3. From these passages, ask them to write a 'mini-theology' of why it 'rains' on people. It doesn't need to be long, but suggest they include:

- ■ **Why?** Reasons from the verses as to why God allows people to face difficulties.
- ■ **Our response.** The importance of our reaction (Job 2:10).
- ■ **Reality.** The reality of bad and good things happening to everyone.

Come back together and ask each group to read out their mini-theologies. Encourage them to keep copies of this for when they are having tough times.

98. BRINGING IN THE KINGDOM

TRACK 6: Turn

LENGTH: 4 mins 24 secs

IN BRIEF: To unpack what the kingdom of God is and the part we have to play in bringing it about.

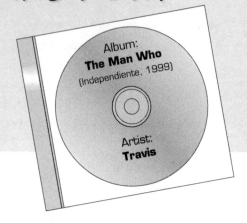

Album:
The Man Who
(Independiente, 1999)

Artist:
Travis

PLAY THE TRACK > > > > >

Ask for people's thoughts on the song's message then say that this song is about the singer's vision of 'the kingdom', a place where he'll belong and feel young and alive. He sees the need for people to 'turn' and change if this is to happen. Jesus came with a similar message.

Ask someone to read out Mark 1:14-15.

Explain that you are going to look at what the Kingdom of God is. Give everyone a sheet of paper and pen, and several minutes to complete the sentence 'My ideal world would be . . . .' Allow time for people to read theirs out.

Old Testament prophets saw the Kingdom of God as like Eden – a place where God would rule, and evil would be overcome

Do a Bible study looking at the Kingdom of God. Ask everyone to draw two vertical lines down their page so that it's divided into three columns. Head the first column **'Characteristics of God's Kingdom'**, the second **'What Needs to Change'** and the third **'Our World'**. As you go through the passages get them to fill in the first column. Use these points as a guide for the Bible study:

- Old Testament prophets saw the Kingdom of God as like Eden – a place where God would rule, and evil would be overcome (Isaiah 29:18-19, Psalm 145:8-11, 1 Chronicles 29:11).

- John the Baptist said the kingdom was 'at hand'. He saw it in the person of Jesus (Matthew 3:2-3).

- Jesus identified the kingdom as soon as he started his ministry (Mark 1:14-15) and saw it as having come through his ministry (Matthew 12:28).

- Jesus always worked towards building it in whatever he did. He called people to have righteousness fit for the kingdom (Matthew 5:20).

- Jesus' acts made sense in the broader picture of the kingdom. Isaiah spoke of the signs of the kingdom (Isaiah 35:5-6) and Jesus defined himself by these signs to John the Baptist (Matthew 11:5).

- Satan's power was broken through the coming of the kingdom (Luke 10:18).

- The future kingdom will come to pass when Christ returns. The present kingdom is building up to that.

PLAY THE TRACK AGAIN> > > > >

After the study, play the track again and ask the group to fill in the third column, 'Our World', by contrasting the characteristics of God's kingdom in the first column with the reality of those things today.

Spend 5 minutes brainstorming what should go in the centre column to move from the reality of our world to the characteristics of God's kingdom.

Invite each person to draw around one of their hands and cut out the shape. Instruct them to fill a characteristic of the kingdom on each finger and then on the other side five things they want to do to bring about that characteristic of the kingdom.

Explain that the way we bring about change is with our hands. These are the tools of the kingdom.

End by praying the Lord's Prayer.

99. GRACE

TRACK 11: Grace

LENGTH: 5 mins 31 secs

IN BRIEF: This session looks at the characteristics of God's grace and what they look like in people.

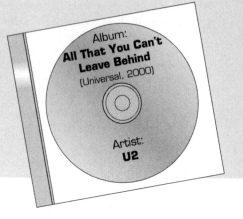

Album:
All That You Can't Leave Behind
(Universal, 2000)

Artist:
U2

APPLICATION

Grace is often viewed as being a passive act by a benevolent God in overlooking the frequent failings of humans. The aim of this session is to highlight that real grace is active and involved in the dirt of real life.

PLAY THE TRACK > > > > >

During the first minute – which is instrumental – say that Jesus didn't talk much about grace. In fact, there is no record of him ever delivering a talk to the disciples on 'grace' or what it means. Listen to the track and think about what grace is and does and what part it had in Jesus' life.

After it has finished, ask the group for comments on, and definitions of grace. Although Jesus didn't talk much about grace, ask them how and where he showed it? (Examples include: Luke 4:40; John 6:12-13; Mark 10:16; Matthew 8:2-3.)

Read out the line from the second verse of the song about grace being a 'thought that changed the world'. Ask the group whether they see grace as a thought, an action or both?

Draw together the discussion by reading Romans 5:18 (from the New Century Version if available) as a definition of grace. Emphasise that grace is shown through the actions of God. It's a word to describe the way in which God acts towards us.

Split the group into three smaller clusters. Each group will be given lyrics to several verses from the song. Based on these, they must come up with a character description of 'Grace' – the person. The song cleverly takes the characteristics of grace and personifies them.

The groups will need to think beyond simply repeating what the lyrics say, and try to come up with a rounded character outline. This will help them understand what Grace looks like in real life. They must apply this into the scenario they will be given and think about how Grace might react in that situation.

- Give the lyrics of the first two verses to one group. Tell them to imagine they have been at a party at a friend's house and things have got out of hand. A window has been smashed and there is drink on the carpet. Some local youths have gate crashed and are brawling. Based on these verses, how does 'Grace' – the person – react?

- Give the second group the lyrics to the third and fourth verses. They must imagine that they are homeless and alone. They are hungry and thirsty and wishing someone would show them some practical love. Based on these verses, how does 'Grace' – the person – act?

- Give the third group the final verse and last line. Each of the group must imagine they have lost a very close friend through a fatal car crash. They are struggling to come to terms with it. What does 'Grace' – the person – do to help?

Allow each group to feed back their ideas. Note down or remember the characteristics of 'Grace' they come up with and try to pull together the meeting by summarising some ways 'Grace' might react in real-life situations.

Challenge each person to think about a situation they are in which requires them either to show grace to others, or to receive grace from God to deal with it. Close by playing the track again and in the first minute read the following:

Grace is a way of acting.
It describes the way God acts towards us.
It describes the way God's followers act towards each other.
It describes the way God's followers act in society.
Grace is a thought and an action.
It's the difference between leaving an ugly situation ugly
and turning something ugly into something beautiful.

Grace is the difference between leaving an ugly situation ugly and turning something ugly into something beautiful

100. PEACE ON EARTH

TRACK 8: Peace on Earth

LENGTH: 4 mins 46 secs

IN BRIEF: A look at how elusive and complicated world peace seems to be, and at how Jesus is Prince of Peace and, at the same time, bringer of justice.

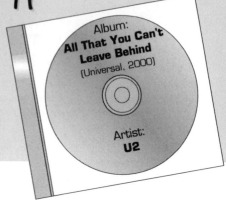

Album:
All That You Can't Leave Behind
(Universal, 2000)

Artist:
U2

APPLICATION

This song represents both a heartfelt cry for some peace across the world and a call for Jesus to intervene. It would make an excellent introduction to a session on issues of global unrest, the bloody reality of war and whether peace is possible.

Search the Internet for images of war-torn areas. Have these either displayed on screens or printed off.

PLAY THE TRACK > > > > >

Play the track, and as it finishes read out the last verse and last three lines from the CD inlay. Use this as the basis for the meeting: Is peace on earth possible?

Start by introducing the ideas of peace and justice. Say that Jesus was described as the Prince of Peace, yet he is also depicted as the one who will grant justice to the nations (Matthew 12:18-21). Do these two things conflict? How can he be both?

Read out the following scenario and let the group wrestle with the idea that in certain situations peace comes with a price tag which may be too big, and justice may be more important than peace:

A dictator has wiped out thousands of his own people who he perceived as posing a threat to his regime. Their families are hungry for justice, which would be likely to involve a neighbouring power invading to unseat the dictator. The rest of the country, however, are keen to see a level of peace and normality restored to their lives, believing that the power-thirsty leader is not seeking to spill anyone else's blood.

Divide the group in half. Ask one group to imagine that they are the families of the victims and the other to play the part of those preferring peace at any price. Give them 5 minutes to prepare a presentation of their recommended action. Give both groups Leviticus 26:1-6 to read and consider as part of this exercise.

PLAY THE TRACK AGAIN > > > > >

End by playing the track again. Invite the group to listen carefully to the first verse and consider whether they think it is:

- ■ too idealistic and a bit naïve.
- ■ helpfully idealistic and raising expectations.
- ■ something they think can happen.

Close by praying for peace on earth and bring it back home – praying for peace in our own lives and actions.

In certain situations peace comes with a price tag which may be too big

INDEX